The Labor Market as a Social Institution

The Royer Lectures

Series editor: John M. Letiche, University of
California, Berkeley

The Labor Market as a Social Institution

Robert M. Solow

Basil Blackwell

First published 1990

Basil Blackwell, Inc.
3 Cambridge Center
Cambridge, Massachusetts 02142, USA

Basil Blackwell Ltd
108 Cowley Road, Oxford, OX4 1JF, UK

Library of Congress Cataloging in Publication Data

Solow, Robert M.
   The labor market as a social institution / Robert M. Solow.
     p. cm.
   Includes bibliographical references.
   ISBN 1–55786–086–6
   1. Labor market. 2. Social institutions. I. Title.
HD5707.S624 1990
306.3′6–dc20   89–18648
                                                CIP

British Library Cataloguing in Publication Data

A CIP catalogue record for this book is available from the British Library.

Typeset in 12 on 14 pt Times
by Photo·graphics, Honiton, East Devon
Printed in Great Britain by Billing & Sons Ltd, Worcester

Contents

Foreword

This book is a gem. Nobel laureate Robert M. Solow has made a fundamental contribution to the analysis of the labor market as a social institution, including its implications for policy in the United States and Western Europe. It is path-breaking in its analysis by demonstrating the existence of a *range* of equilibria with regard to high and persistent unemployment. In a lively style, Solow argues convincingly that the current textbook explanations of mass unemployment are erroneous and misleading.

He urges that traditional economic theories, with the standard collection of categories, have misinterpreted the working of the labor market and consequently have failed to explain the relative inflexibility of wages and the persistence of high unemployment. The customary labor–leisure analysis, Solow indicates, has taken account of technological and budgetary constraints, but it has seriously ignored the constraints arising from social norms, especially those of *fairness* that constitute an important ingredient in the actual operation of labor markets. Solow therefore emphasizes the need to recognize, analytically, that wage rates affect the

quality and intensity of work, and hence the productivity of labor. His marshalling of evidence on this point is a real contribution to the history of labor economics. Under the rubric of "Circumstantial Evidence," he cites corroborative statements by distinguished economists ranging from Sir Henry Clay, Alfred Marshall, and Arthur C. Pigou to Sir John R. Hicks, Clark Kerr, Paul Pigors, and Charles Myers. Further, Solow draws on the substantive reports of the Manpower Development Research Corporation of New York and of the Illinois Reemployment Bonus Experiments. With illuminating brevity, he then incorporates the most recent and cogent macroeconomic literature into the analysis.

Changes in the assumptions of traditional labor market theorizing, he shows, are ineluctably required, changes recognizing that wages and jobs are significantly different from other prices and quantities. It is profitability, establishment size, and capital intensity that seem to be the industrial correlates of high wages. "These regularities," Solow writes, "are generally supportive of the notion that wages arise as an outcome of bargaining over rents" (p. 27). His analysis of the causation of modern persistent unemployment is developed in a general equilibrium approach, within which the fundamental issue is to show that following social norms is individually rational for both wage earners and employers. The efficiency–wage and the insider–outsider approaches, he demonstrates, contain important insights, but leave very significant gaps to be filled.

As for the efficiency approach, all the discipline is assumed to occur via the threat of unemployment, and the performance of the worker is influenced by the wage rate. Supply and demand analysis in the usual efficiency way, however, is inadequate here: for the wage cannot perfectly perform the role of both a simple cost and a productive factor. It is precisely the character of the labor market as a social institution – with different evaluations by employer and employee of performance – that may make it generate an inefficiently low level of employment. As regards the insider–outsider approach, it is assumed that the insiders are experienced workers who generate a substantial rent jointly with the rest of the apparatus of the firm. If they are successful in keeping the unemployed out, they can bargain for the resulting rent with the employers. In consequence, they can achieve a wage bargain higher than the level that would allow the firm profitably to employ a substantial number of the unemployed outsiders. Involuntary unemployment could therefore persist, but it would not be an equilibrium as the unemployed would bid for jobs. The kind of labor market usually underlying the textbook approaches would, in effect, be consistent with this argument. However, one of the important and original contributions of Solow's analysis centers in an examination of the reasons why employers would generally tend to reject competitive efforts by the unemployed to undercut the going wage rate. With the unemployed willing but unable to undercut, involuntary unemployment would clearly persist.

Even more fundamental, Solow shows that under contemporary conditions in developed market economies, for a certain range, neither employers nor unemployed, as a group, would wish to resort to undercutting. In such circumstances, which currently are pervasive, mass unemployment could certainly persist with equilibrium conditions in the labor market.

Brilliantly, Solow applies the concepts of the "prisoner's dilemma" to the problem of sustained unemployment. Though the rejection of undercutting may be at least mildly disadvantageous to the individual unemployed, Solow observes that the lack of massive undercutting becomes the social norm. Some conflict between the private and social consequences of actions is probably a necessary part of the social condition. Otherwise, Solow notes, there would be no need for a special code. In time, the institutionalization of social norms begins to emerge, with people doing something because it is the right thing rather than because they have "reckoned" precisely all the consequences (p. 43).

Abnormal conditions aside, Solow suggests that wage earners may be said to have a reservation wage below which they would not accept employment. Generally, the lower limit would obtain if they were unemployed and on the dole. In the extraordinary situation where the unemployed paid no attention whatsoever to the future, it would be logical for them to attempt to undercut the existing wage. More generally, however, for any given rate of discounting the future by wage earners there would be a range

of wage rates between the going wage and being on the dole, any one of which could be an equilibrium wage with accompanying persistent unemployment. The avoidance of widespread undercutting, Solow submits, has been brought about not only by the existence of social norms buttressed by all forms of unemployment benefits, but also by the threat of "Hobbesian competition." This form of competition would entail a punishment strategy both by the remaining unemployed and by the employed, leaving all in a "brutish" state. It is therefore a strategy that serves the purpose of enforcing the equilibrium with persistent unemployment and without significant wage undercutting. Solow presents his analysis not as a literal description of reality, but as an "extended metaphor" (p. 48), an approach for analyzing the perceived conditions of sticky wages and often persistently high unemployment in North America and Western Europe.

Experience and reason seem to confirm his confidence in the emergence of social norms that become internalized. Among the important results of his analysis is the doubt cast on the empirical reliability and stability imputed to so-called "natural" rates of unemployment, and the demonstration of the possible existence of equilibrium with a range of unemployment rates and wage levels. This approach points the way toward lowering the unemployment rate by improving the operation of labor markets.

Econometric tests for the United States show that in the period 1955–86 wage acceleration more or less vanished whenever the unemployment rate was

approximately where it had been for the previous 5 years. "Path dependence, if you take it seriously," Solow concludes, "implies its own kind of world, but it is a world that has a logic of its own" (p. 87). Indeed, the reasonableness of his approach for fresh theoretical–quantitative work would appear to be matched only by its discernible promise for public policy.

Though the United States has perhaps been the best case to support the idea of a stable equilibrium unemployment rate – somewhat below 5.5 percent – according to Solow's analysis, there appears to be only weak support even for this view. US experience since Solow delivered his lectures seems to give further support to his argument. Even the simplest representation of his view that the labor market is largely norm guided gives nearly as good an account of the US data. As for Western Europe, the attempt to salvage the idea of a well-defined equilibrium unemployment rate has required "the equilibrium rate" to have undergone drastic change between the 1970s and the 1980s, hardly an acceptable procedure for solid analysis or credible policy. Contrariwise, Solow's approach provides a new technique for testing reasonable models of norm-guided labor markets. It opens up possibilities that the standard view simply suppresses. For, in Solow's approach, history matters; it provides the opportunity to use the best available "tooled knowledge" for analyzing the reasons why the unemployment rate may have been permitted to drift to the top of its equilibrium range, and what policies would be most likely to

lower it. His approach, furthermore, pertains not to the old notion of a permanent trade-off between inflation and unemployment, but to the permanent increase, if any, in inflation as the cost of getting from a high unemployment rate to a lower one. This distinction makes a new kind of case for many forms of public policy. When the goal is to *reduce* the unemployment rate from the top of an equilibrium range to a lower one, a temporary incomes policy might be effective. If *acceleration* of inflation could be eliminated during the transition, the situation at the end of the period should be just as viable as the situation at the beginning – so long as the unemployment rate remains in the equilibrium range. Solow devotes ample attention to the risks involved in attempting to implement such a policy, but he suggests that the smaller North European economies may have recently achieved some of these objectives (p. 75); see also Lars Calmfors, "Wage Formation and Macroeconomic Policy in the Nordic Countries," in *Wage Formation in the Nordic Countries* (to be published by SNS, Stockholm, 1990), chapter 1, and Assar Lindbeck, "Unemployment and Labor Market Imperfections" (mimeo, Institute for International Economic Studies, University of Stockholm, August 1989).

Solow confines his "Implications for Practice" to recommendations that follow strictly from his analytical framework. He considers institutional reforms as a way of shifting the range of equilibrium unemployment rates downward. Accordingly, he suggests ways of strengthening the voice of unem-

ployed "outsiders" via improved representation in labor unions. Where the efficiency–wage argument may be relevant, some compensation for work tied to group effort or group activity, he proposes, might be incorporated into current compensation schemes and provide additional benefits for all concerned. Certain sophisticated compensation schemes with a significant profit-sharing component, he notes, might also help to lower the range of equilibrium unemployment rates. Apart from these effects, Solow draws attention to the more general growing evidence that there has been too little emphasis on teamwork and too much emphasis on individual performance in recent American industrial behavior for its own good at all levels.

On the supply side of labor, Solow thinks that the social norm against "unfair" wage competition could emerge as a reinforcement of a particular equilibrium choice of strategies for both wage earners and employers. In that equilibrium, abstention from wage undercutting would be enforced by the latent threat of reversion to Hobbesian competition. Moreover, he observes that attempts to improve the working of the labor market by making it more nearly "perfectly competitive" may be misguided in two respects. First, these attempts may logically be resisted by both the wage earners and the employers, and hence rendered impractical. Second, they may not be in the best interests of wage earners who might be willing to pay a price to avoid having their livelihood governed by atomistic competition. Therefore the achievement of wage flexibility

through unrestricted competition might not be in the best interests of either the wage earners or the employers. The fundamental question, Solow writes, is can we improve the labor–market institutions "so that they can provide the job security and wage continuity that people seem to want, without falling into . . . that grossest inefficiency – persistent unemployment" (p. 80).

Two appendices furnish mathematical and econometric support for important arguments made in the text. They are clarifying, not forbidding. Bibliographical Notes following each chapter contain the documentation of sources cited in the text and commentaries on the·most relevant related literature.

Members of the Department of Economics at the University of California at Berkeley are deeply pleased to have had Professor Robert M. Solow deliver the 1989 Royer Lectures, upon which this book is based. We hope the reader will have occasion to share our gratitude for his significant contribution and our obligation to the publishers for expediting publication.

John M. Letiche

Preface

One of the first economics courses I attended as an undergraduate some 50 years ago was John Dunlop's on labor economics. Ever since then, a lot of my best friends have been labor economists. Maybe that is why it has long been a source of nagging intellectual discomfort for me that the treatment of the labor market by macroeconomic theorists is so much at variance with the beliefs of those who study it most closely.

I understand perfectly well that it is not the job of theory to get the details right. A map on the scale of one inch to the mile does not show every bend in the road. But you expect the general directions to be right; and you expect the map to distinguish correctly between a six-lane divided highway and a dirt road. The labor market plays a prominent role in most macro-models: the wage bill is a large fraction of national income, and unemployment is an important pathology in its own right as well as a signal of general economic slack. Yet in today's preferred style the labor market is usually modelled as just clearing or, more subtly, producing efficient contracts. Bits of realism appear

here and there in the literature but have not made
much headway. You do not have to be a congenital
skeptic to doubt that this sort of map gives a useful
picture of the lay of the land.

Anyone would be flattered by an invitation from
a great university to deliver these lectures in the
footsteps of Theodore Schultz, Lawrence Klein,
Edmond Malinvaud and Amartya Sen. I was not
quite flattered enough to believe that a potpourri of
my own recent research interests would be an
adequate response. So I decided to try a sketch of
my own doubts and affirmations about the labor
market, as a small contribution to the reform of
macroeconomic theory. My hope was to communi-
cate both to economists who, even if they do not
participate in this particular debate, are important
spectators, and to other social scientists who are
often bemused by what they hear coming from
economics and wonder if there is something intrinsic
to the discipline that requires it to fly in the face of
common sense. The result is what you see.

During my lifetime I have listened to hundreds of
public lectures by economists and other scholars of
all degrees of distinction. I do not remember a single
one that seemed too short. In preparing these
lectures I tried very hard to keep each one down to
the scant academic hour. And I have resisted the
temptation to doll them up for publication. I have
added a Bibliographical Note to each lecture as a
substitute for footnotes, and a brief Appendix to
each of the last two lectures to justify some mildly
technical statements made in the text. Otherwise

these are the lectures as I delivered them in Berkeley.

I would like to thank the University of California at Berkeley for the honor of an invitation to be Royer Lecturer, and my friends in the Department of Economics for the warmth of their welcome during the week we spent there. My wife and I owe a special word of gratitude to Jack and Emily Letiche for being hosts of superb care and delicacy. I am grateful to Aase Huggins and Eva Hakala who typed the manuscript with their usual efficiency and good humor. My thanks go also to Ms Sabina Ahmed and Ms Li-Lin Goh, my undergraduate research assistants at the Massachusetts Institute of Technology, who carried out the statistical work described in the last lecture with skill and enthusiasm.

1 Circumstantial Evidence

I want to sidle up to my subject indirectly by first saying something about the relationship of academic scholarship to common sense. On the whole, scholars enjoy confuting common sense. They like to show that what "everyone thinks" is all wrong. We all take obvious pleasure in creating a sensation by nonplussing the conventional wisdom. It feeds our sense of doing something of value. You can see this happening in subjects as diverse as history and astronomy. There is particular pleasure in demonstrating that Thomas Jefferson was not a virtuous man, or that there are objects, like black holes, with amazing properties. So also in economics.

Maybe even more so in economics. There is more folk wisdom going around about economics than there is about biology or chemistry and so naturally there are more opportunities to put down common sense. Often, maybe even usually, the confrontation with common sense is successful. Take for example the "paradox of thrift," the Keynesian demonstration that, when aggregate output is limited by effective demand, an attempt to create an autonomous increase in saving may, if successful, diminish the

total of saving. I realize that there are many economists today who think that Keynes's argument was all wrong and common sense was right; I do not presume to settle that issue, only to point out that for a quarter-century the refutation of common sense stood. You can recall other examples; think about tariffs.

There is an important difference, however, between natural science and social science when it comes to the status of common sense. It does not matter what the person in the street believes about the nature of condensed matter or the movements of heavenly bodies. The same experiments on superconductivity will be performed and the same astronomical measurements will be made, and they will come out the same way, no matter what "people" think. (Leave aside the question whether public funds will be made available for unpopular research. Peer review was invented for that contingency.) In economics, however, the common-sense beliefs of businessmen, bankers, workers, managers, con-sumers, and speculators affect how they interpret what they see and therefore affect what they do. Common-sense beliefs about the economy are therefore an important influence on the behavior of the economy. They may even be decisive for what is actually true about it (as with the effects of a monetary injection). For the same reason, one might be inclined to take common-sense beliefs about the economy more seriously than common-sense beliefs about superconducting materials. When "people" think this or that about the economy, they are in

part thinking about themselves. Even if they are not always right about themselves (let alone about the economic system), they could be said to have a certain privileged position.

These abstract remarks have some particular relevance because my general subject in these lectures is the right way to think about the labor market, or at least about two or three aspects of the labor market. One important tradition within economics, perhaps the dominant tradition right now, especially in macroeconomics, holds that in nearly all respects the labor market is just like other markets. It should be analyzed in much the same way that one would analyze the market for any perishable commodity, using the conventional apparatus of supply and demand. Common sense, on the other hand, seems to take it for granted that there is something special about labor as a commodity, and therefore about the labor market too. (It is not hard to see why one might think that. It is worth pointing out that specialists in labor economics and industrial relations tend to side with common sense in this instance.)

In the rest of this lecture I want to make the case that the labor market really is different. In particular, I claim that it cannot be understood without taking account of the fact that participants, on both sides, have well-developed notions of what is fair and what is not. In trying to convince you I will make use of all the rhetorical tricks. I will appeal to authority, I will appeal to common sense, I will produce a few relevant facts, especially ones that I hope you have

not heard about before.

If there are any civilians here they will wonder why I spend so much time and effort, and exhibit so much defensiveness, in asserting the obvious. I have already explained why. Among economists, it is not obvious at all that labor as a commodity is sufficiently different from artichokes and rental apartments to require a different mode of analysis. In fact many economists will regard this idea as simply bizarre. I have some faint hope that Berkeley economists may have been softened up by exposure to the work of Professor George Akerlof and Professor Janet Yellen, whose ideas are a lot like mine (though I will on purpose emphasize somewhat different ways of examining the question).

In the second lecture I will focus on what has always seemed to me to be one of the main puzzles about the labor market and one of the main reasons for doubting the validity of the standard view. That is: when there is a non-trivial amount of unemployment, why is there not active competition for the limited number of jobs, and why does that competition not force wages down quite promptly? That is what we expect from artichokes and rental apartments, and it is roughly what we get. You will see at once how a notion of fairness and a related standard of acceptable behavior might provide a solution to the puzzle. But that loose implication will hardly do by itself. For one thing, it is too easy, too close to the surface, to be academically respectable. So I will try to provide a model, a sort of semi-formalization, of the way in which such a

standard might arise and be maintained through thick and thin (at least if it is not too thin).

Finally, in the third lecture, I will try to relate all this to some more immediate and practical pieces of modern macroeconomics. First of all, I will try to undermine the notion of a stable "natural rate of unemployment." I put it tentatively like that because I am not at all sure what the right theory is for that situation. But I am fairly confident that the "natural rate" theory has been given more widespread acceptance than it has earned. So I will use the notions discussed in the first two lectures, plus some empirical work by myself and others, to infiltrate some skepticism about the theory and its policy implications. Then I will say a little about the policy notions that might follow from the view of unemployment proposed here.

The most elementary reason for thinking that the concept of fairness, and beliefs about what is fair and what is not, play an important part in labor-market behavior is that we talk about them all the time. That is the appeal to common sense. The fact is so obvious that I will not trouble you with examples, except to bet that if you conjure up in your mind a picture of a picket line, the largest word on the placards is likely to be "UNFAIR." Let me quote from an essay called "A Fair Rate of Wages" by no less a person than Alfred Marshall. He says ". . . the phrase is constantly used in the market place; it is frequent in the mouths both of employers and the employed; and almost every

phrase in common use has a real meaning, though
it may be difficult to get at." (Full documentation
is provided in the Bibliographical Notes to each
lecture. This reference is to page 212.) I am going
to return to Marshall's essay later. It was called to
my attention by Professor R.C.O. Matthews, which
seems appropriate because he is the current tenant
of the professorship at Cambridge once held by
Marshall.

A few days after writing these lines I walked past
a group of picketing painters. The word "UNFAIR"
was not to be seen. I was disappointed. When I
looked again at the signs, I saw that they said that
the X Construction Company "does not observe
COMMUNITY STANDARDS in wages and working conditions." It made my day. From the point of
view of these lectures, there is no better definition
of "unfair."

Of course it is conceivable that a phrase or concept
that is in everyone's mouth, or even in everyone's
brain, should have nothing to do with the reality of
outcomes. They may be words, just words, as
Kenneth Burke once said of the novel. That seems
especially implausible in a context like the labor
market where negotiation and bargaining play a
fairly conspicuous role. But it is hard to give a
conclusive proof of the opposite. Even if the
employers and the employed who talk about fairness
are not just cynical phonies, their decisions may be
entirely controlled by an invisible force, whether
they know it or not. All one can do is to offer
circumstantial evidence, which is what I try in this

lecture, and to show that the view that I am advocating can explain things that the alternative view cannot – I try that in the next lecture.

Perhaps it is worth pointing out explicitly that talk about fairness crops up in markets for ordinary material goods too. Resale price maintenance is usually called "fair trade" presumably for a reason. I do not have to remind you of the ancient notion of the "just price." Wherever buyers and sellers have a durable relationship, the idea of fair treatment is likely to make an appearance, as Arthur Okun argued some years ago. Nevertheless one suspects that it is likely to be more ubiquitous and more effective in the labor market, for reasons that are not far from the surface.

A second reason for believing that norms of equity and fairness have an effective – and not merely an emotive or symbolic – function in the labor market is that they turn up frequently and prominently in the literature of industrial relations and personnel management. Manuals for the training of people who actually engage in wage setting and wage negotiation teach practitioners that equity and perceived equity, over time and across occupations and firms, are an indispensable characteristic of a good system of industrial relations. Otherwise there will be quits, low morale and accompanying low productivity. Observers of industrial relations confirm this. It seems quite unreasonable to suppose that such statements are just deceptive cover-ups for unrestrained gouging.

I could offer you several samples of the sort of

thing that personnel managers are taught. But there are adequate references in the works of Akerlof and Yellen and of the French economist Serge Kolm (who cites both French and English texts) so that it is not necessary for me to pile up more evidence. The temptation is irresistible, however, to offer you two quotations. The first is from Clark Kerr (in an essay on "Labor Markets: Their Character and Consequences" of 1950) and the second is from my own former colleagues Paul Pigors and Charles Myers (in their standard textbook *Personnel Administration*, last reprinted in 1977).

> Sir Henry Clay has noted that in England before World War I, "wages, it may fairly be said, constituted a system, since there were well understood rates for most occupations; the relations between these were stable and generally accepted, and a change in any one rate would prompt demands for a change in other rates". This "system" resulted, in part, from commonly accepted rules of equity and from institutional controls. Both militate against economic forces which tend to pull the system apart. As institutional controls spread and deepen, the "system" may become increasingly formalized with "historical relations" and "patterns" taking the place more and more of supply and demand . . . . It may eventually appear that the "system of wages" will have to be regarded as an independent variable, rather than as a dependent variable at the mercy of a myriad of economic forces.

From Pigors and Myers: "Wage and salary differentials are a mark of social status in almost every

organization. If they do not correspond to the relative significance of jobs, as employees view them, the employee's sense of justice is outraged."

They then quote from a release of the War Labor Board in 1943: "There is no single factor in the whole field of labor relations that does more to break down morale, create individual dissatisfaction, encourage absenteeism, increase labor turnover, and hamper productivity than obviously unjust inequalities paid to different individuals in the same labor group within the same plant." Pigors and Myers enlarge the scope of this argument to firms in the same or other communities.

The fundamental reason for believing that fairness is a factor in labor markets is what we know about our own society and its culture. Bear in mind that I am speaking now as an ordinary citizen-observer, not as someone with professional knowledge or expertise, though I will in a moment return to report information I have come by more honestly.

We live in a society in which social status and self-esteem are strongly tied both to occupation and income. Of course occupation and income are correlated, but not perfectly correlated. It seems undeniable to me that both occupation and income are significant variables. The way others look at us, and the way we look at ourselves, are both income related, and both are job related at given income. Employment and the income it brings are not simply *equivalent* to a set of bundles of consumer goods (and savings). But that is exactly the way textbook economics treats them. I am ignoring the disutility

of labor here, but only because all my sentences would get longer and more complicated if I took account of that. Nor is it of any great importance for the point I am trying to make that consumer goods may have relations of complementarity and substitutability with hours of different kinds of labor. (Treat that fact as the basis for a possible exam question.)

Once you admit to yourself that wage rates and employment are profoundly entwined with social status and self-esteem you have already left the textbook treatment of the labor market behind. We all want to be treated as we deserve to be treated, or perhaps better. When Rodney Dangerfield tells you that he "don't get no respect," it is all too obvious that the fact wounds him. To say that we want to be treated fairly is almost tautological; fairness is what we are entitled to. In whatever concerns my employment and my pay, issues of fairness will play a part, along with issues of budget feasibility.

That is about as much deep sociological thought as I can manage. I turn now to some bodies of evidence that seem to bear, positively or negatively, directly or indirectly, on the adequacy of the simple textbook treatment of employment.

The first of these is negative in its implications, serving to show that the conventional, purely pecuniary, factors have very little explanatory power even at the micro-level. My source is a paper by Bruce Meyer of Northwestern University (see page 25).

In 1984, the State of Illinois operated an experiment designed to test the effectiveness of financial incentives in inducing recipients of unemployment insurance benefits to find jobs more quickly. Eligibles were assigned randomly to a control group or to one of two experimental treatments. I will describe only the simpler of these; the other gave similar results. Experimental subjects were offered a $500 bonus if they became employed after no more than 10 weeks of benefits and held on to the job for 4 months; otherwise the normal rules applied. The effects of the bonus scheme are measured by comparison with the control group.

The results can be summarized by three statements. First, experimentals did have a generally higher probability of leaving unemployment than the controls did, but the effect was pretty small: the length of that spell of unemployment was reduced from an average of 18.3 weeks to 17.0 weeks. The difference is statistically significant. Secondly, although the textbook analysis of labor–leisure choice suggests that the incentive effect of the bonus ought to have a major bulge in the week or two before its availability expires, this effect is not reliably observed. There is a tendency for the reemployment probability of experimentals to exceed that of controls by an extra amount in the last 2 weeks of eligibility, but the difference is small and is not statistically significant. Finally, the same textbook analysis suggests that the incentive effect of the bonus ought to be considerably larger for

those with lower earning capacity. No such effect is observed. It should be mentioned explicitly that the size of the bonus is not trivial; it amounts to about $2\frac{1}{2}$ weeks of earnings for the median claimant of unemployment insurance benefit, and therefore surely to much more for the subgroup with the lowest earnings when employed.

Meyer concludes that "the results of the experiments call into question the applicability of the standard labor–leisure model for describing unemployment." (Similar conclusions apply to the usual sort of search model of unemployment, but it would take me too far afield to go into that. The implications are much the same for the general point I am after.) The employment and job-search choices of unemployed workers, so far as they have choices, do not seem to be governed simply, or even predominantly, by any simple trade between income and the irksomeness of labor. There must be other considerations operating. These experiments provide no information about what those other considerations might be, but they should leave one open-minded.

Now I turn to another source of indirect evidence, also peripheral to the main issue but revealing nevertheless. The results to which I will refer are a by-product of initiatives taken by several States (including California) to combine public assistance – welfare – with work. The fact that there is such persistent political pressure in this direction is itself instructive. The wish to combine welfare with work, or to replace welfare by work, is not only persistent but also diverse. Some of it is punitive in character,

and much of that is no doubt racist. Some of it is aimed more benevolently against what is perceived to be a culture of welfare, unproductive even for its participants. Some of it is incentive oriented, seeking to induce or drive people away from public assistance. But some of it is clearly motivated by the feeling that welfare is *unfair* to the working poor. There are many people with full-time or long part-time jobs whose earnings amount to no more than, or not much more than, the size of the public assistance package that can be put together in the richer states. This seems inequitable to them and even to others. Requiring welfare recipients to work off their grants, if they are not disabled or occupied with small children, seems to be a way of restoring equity without inflicting hardship.

I do not want to argue whether the perception of inequity is correct, or whether workfare is a valid remedy. It only matters that the perception is there. It is not my main point anyway. The fact is that the Omnibus Budget Reconciliation Act of 1981, while reducing aggregate funding for public assistance, also authorized states to experiment with work–welfare schemes and allowed use of Federal funds for this purpose. A number of states chose to field experiments along that line. The Manpower Demonstration Research Corporation (MDRC) of New York (not for profit) helped to design, organize and operate a dozen of these, and has analyzed the results. The main goals of analysis are to study the feasibility of work–welfare programs and to estimate their effects on participants and their costs and

benefits to society and its segments. But there is also some material that is useful for my purpose here.

States devised a variety of programs. Some of them had the feature that eligible participants were required to work off their welfare grants in jobs at public or private not-for-profit agencies, almost always at the statutory minimum wage. In the course of studying the large-scale feasibility of such programs, MDRC collected information about the attitudes of workfare participants and their supervisors. That is what I want to tell you about.

The jobs provided under the various programs were hardly cushy. On the manual side they were mostly mopping and sweeping; on the clerical side, elementary filing would be typical. Nevertheless, a little over 70 percent of participants reported that they were satisfied to receive their benefits tied to a job, as compared with just receiving the benefits. This is not particularly germane to the central point; but if I want to make a fuss about the ethical aspects of work, it may be relevant to document that the work ethic is alive and well.

Nor were the jobs phony make-work, as far as one can tell. Participants and their supervisors seemed to agree. About 90 percent of each group described the work being done as necessary to the agency. This is one of those cases where the belief is probably more important than the actuality. If the desire to see oneself as a significant contributor is strong, any event that denies one's significance is

likely to be resisted, and the resistance is a way of affirming the significance.

Finally, participants in the programs were asked to compare the usefulness of their work with the amount of money they were receiving in return. On average, three-quarters of those interviewed thought that the employing agency was getting the better end of the deal; 15 percent thought that they were getting the better deal; and the remaining 10 percent called it even. The proportions varied from state to state and the differences may even bear some relation to the reality of the underlying situations. No matter. I do not know if hope springs eternal in the human breast; the feeling of being underpaid pretty clearly does so.

The MDRC studies of state work–welfare initiatives are full of interest in their own right, and they contain information of great value for the design of welfare reform and social policy more generally. That is not my particular interest here. Neither is the simple fact that so many of the mothers receiving Aid to Families with Dependent Children (AFDC) clearly preferred work to straight welfare, though that is hardly irrelevant to an understanding of the role of employment in our society. But I want to underline a different aspect of these reports.

Remember that the participants in these experiments were generally under-educated. (Only half had graduated from high school.) They had very little work experience, and certainly very little successful work experience. Most had long histories

of AFDC dependence, and well under half had
held a job in the 2 years before the experiment.
Nevertheless their evaluation of their own performance, and of their contributions to the employing
agency, were generally quite high. There is clearly
an extraordinarily strong drive to believe that the
laborer is worthy of her hire. It does not even matter
very much whether the self-evaluations are accurate.
They may be; they are generally confirmed by the
supervisors. That is not conclusive. The supervisors,
like the subjects, may be exhibiting the famous
Hawthorne effect (the observed tendency to respond
to attention by feeling and being more productive)
or they may share the drive I imputed to the
participants. What matters from my point of view is
the obviously powerful investment of the workers
in the belief that they *deserve* their earnings. Actually
the shared belief is even sharper. Most of the
participants report that they feel underpaid. They
believe that the employer got the better end of the
bargain. Don't we all feel the same way?

Now I want to come back to Alfred Marshall's
discussion of a fair rate of wages. First let me quote
at length, from page 213 and then 217, for the flavor
as well as the substance.

The basis of the notion that there should be given
"a fair day's wage for a fair day's work" is that
every man who is up to the usual standard of
efficiency of his trade in his own neighborhood, and
exerts himself honestly, ought to be paid for
his work at the usual rate for his trade and

neighbourhood; so that he may be able to live in that way to which he and his neighbors in his rank of life have been accustomed. And further, the popular notion of fairness demands that he should be paid this rate ungrudgingly; that his time should not be taken up in fighting for it; and that he should not be worried by constant attempts to screw his pay down by indirect means. This doctrine is modified by the admission that changes of circumstance may require changes of wages in one direction or another.

That last qualification reminds us that Marshall is not about to forget supply and demand. Nor should we. But it would be a miscalculation to take the qualification as a tacit repudiation of the sentences that went before. Later on, Marshall describes what he thinks happens or ought to happen when market conditions fluctuate. Take the case that product demand increases. "As a general rule employers will be bound in fairness to yield at once in such a case a considerable part of their new profits in higher wages," without waiting to be compelled to do so by industrial action of any kind. In the other direction: "Fairness requires a similar moderation on the part of the employed."

Marshall makes it plain (page 214) that employers are not supposed to take advantage of increases in their own bargaining power that come about because employment is irregular and workers are short of money. More generally, an employer "acts unfairly if he endeavours to make his profits not so much by able and energetic management of his business

as by paying his labor at a lower rate than his competitors; if he takes advantage of the necessities of individual workers, and perhaps of their ignorance of what is going on elsewhere; if he screws a little here and a little there; and perhaps in the course of doing this makes it more difficult for other employers in the same trade to go on paying straightforwardly the full rates." By the way, since it may be hard at any time to know exactly what the appropriate wage rate is, a natural point of reference is the rate paid in some normal recent year. Marshall comes awfully close to suggesting that fair wages will be sticky wages.

It is pretty clear from his language that Marshall is not claiming to describe the way wages are actually determined in England in the 1880s. In fact he argues that trade unionism arises as a natural response to the behavior of employers who are unfair in the sense he has defined. Combativeness is a sign of unfairness. But it is equally clear that he does not think of himself as describing a sort of distant goal or Utopia. He thinks that the tendency of men to want and employers to offer fair treatment plays a significant part in the operation of the labor market then and there. He also approves of it.

As a last piece of anecdotal evidence, I want to summarize a description of the contemporary Swiss labor market by two Swiss economists (J.-P. Danthine and J.-C. Lambelet). Switzerland is not a large or important economy, but it is a useful example precisely because it has an extraordinary record of industrial peace combined with a reputation for strict

adherence to free-market principles and policies. Indeed Danthine and Lambelet describe it as a "context of conservative policies, lightweight public sector and cooperative labor relations."

The labor market is characterized by about a thousand collective bargaining agreements, "many of them defining only the main principles and procedures of negotiation, but not how wages are determined." Wages are actually set at the local level by negotiation which may cover both union and non-union employees. The Swiss observers "think it fruitful on an analytical level to view the Swiss labor scene as a set of numerous bilateral monopolies, generally at the firm level. Both sides basically find themselves in a bilateral prisoner's dilemma-game type of situation, the game being played repeatedly, with no finite time horizon and with no possibility for players to 'kill' their opposite number. Therefore, the recent analysis . . . of the emergence and evolution of *cooperation* as the dominant strategy under these circumstances would seem to apply nicely."

I will come back in the next lecture to the suggestion that labor-market institutions might emerge as a cooperative way for the parties to evade the trap of a prisoner's dilemma. For now I will stick to Danthine's and Lambelet's more direct observations on the functioning of the Swiss labor market.

The evidence – statistical and anecdotal – suggests to them the following scheme. If the demand for Swiss-made goods deteriorates – easy enough to

imagine in an export-oriented economy – the first recourse of labor and management is wage and profit moderation. Real wages are pretty flexible, even in the short run, but the flexibility seems to follow Marshall's injunction that the burden of adjustment should be shared, with wages more stable than profits. The second response is work-sharing, shortening hours for all a firm's employees. The third possibility is layoffs, but these are apparently a last resort, and then mainly when they can be directed at foreign workers, "outsiders." The key point is that wage reductions and short-time working are reversed when demand recovers, without the need for confrontation.

It all sounds rather more like Marshall's picture of a well-functioning labor market than what we are used to here or in Mrs Thatcher's England. But I think some of the elements can be detected in much of the industrial capitalist world, for reasons that should have emerged from the bits and pieces of circumstantial evidence I have been piecing together.

The Danthine–Lambelet description of the way wages and employment are determined in Switzerland reminds me of one last piece of evidence, this time for the UK. Andrew Oswald and David Blanchflower have analyzed a body of micro-data relating to individual manufacturing firms in Britain. One of their findings, after controlling for every characteristic in sight, is that more profitable firms pay higher wages than less profitable firms to equivalent workers. This contradicts the supply-and-demand model of labor as just another commodity.

In that model, firms hiring in the same labor market would offer equivalent packages of wages and working conditions for equivalent workers. It is barely possible, I must admit, that more profitable firms are hiring better workers than less profitable firms, with some relevant quality differences escaping measurement. Oswald and Blanchflower do not think so, however.

The point of this finding is that it is clearly consistent with Marshall's description of the way the notion of "fairness" operates in the labor market. Workers in a firm seem to have some claim to the "rents" generated by the firm. No doubt they have to bargain for their share – one can see this in the difference between union and non-union firms – but there is little doubt that the Marshallian argument is at work too.

This has been a very difficult lecture for someone like me, whose normal professional activity consists of formulating differential or finite-difference equations and trying to figure out what their solution paths look like. I guess I have been trying to soften you up rather than sell you any particular bill of goods. I will just summarize what I have been trying to get across and where I want to go next.

Economic theory comes to the labor market with its standard collection of categories, and has trouble. It has trouble with the relative inflexibility of wages and with the persistence of unemployment. There are lots of ways to respond to this challenge, ranging from denial that the "facts" are as they seem to be,

all the way to genuine modifications of the standard supply-and-demand apparatus. It is not my purpose to survey the field, though I will have to mention a couple of new developments later on in order to motivate my own pursuit.

In this lecture I have tried to remind you in all sorts of ways of something you already know. Wage rates and jobs are not exactly like other prices and quantities. They are much more deeply involved in the way people see themselves, think about their social status, and evaluate whether they are getting a fair shake out of society. That being so, you would think that the determinants of market decisions and responses to market facts might not always be the conventional ones. Buyers and sellers of labor might not accede to perceived injustice merely because of a little excess supply or demand. It may be possible to redefine supply and demand to take account of actions motivated by feelings about equity or about the limits of acceptable response to changes in the economic environment. No matter: the substance of labor-market theory will have changed.

It does not follow from any of this that the ordinary forces of supply and demand are irrelevant to the labor market, or that we can do without the textbook apparatus altogether. It only follows that they are incomplete and need completing. My own impulse is to preserve the apparatus but change the assumptions in ways that recognize the particularities of the labor market. One possibility – suggested by the phrase about a fair day's wage for a fair day's work – is to recognize that wage rates may affect

the intensity and thus the productivity of labor. That was perhaps the earliest adaptation to be tried out by economic theorists. I will have a word to say about "efficiency–wage theory" in the next lecture, but only tangentially. Serge Kolm has investigated the symmetric suggestion that the wage rate might be incorporated in the typical utility function. (If the laborer is worthy of her hire, then a higher wage, implying a higher worth, might have unusual implications.)

Sometimes it seems to me that a more sociological and less psychological way of understanding behavior in labor markets might be suitable. Social institutions define acceptable and unacceptable modes of behavior in weighty contexts like the labor market. Norms of behavior can be modelled as constraints on decisions. They affect behavior whenever they bind. From this point of view, the trouble with the everyday textbook labor–leisure analysis is that it takes account only of technological and budget constraints and ignores the constraints arising from social norms.

You will notice that I have not uttered the dread P-word, paradigm. That is because, to my way of thinking, none of this is radically subversive of mainstream economic theory. In fact I would describe it as methodologically conservative, in the same sense that Franklin Roosevelt's New Deal legislation was conservative despite its hostile reception by the official conservatives of the time. He was trying – effectively or ineffectively – to save capitalism from its worst excesses. To compare great things to small,

it is not a favor to mainstream economics to impose limitations on it that prevent it from dealing intelligently with phenomena so pervasive and basic as inflexible wages and persistent unemployment. I will try to make a little headway in that direction in the next lecture.

Bibliographical Note

Further bits of circumstantial evidence, together with some references to the literature of psychology and sociology, can be found in an unpublished paper by George A. Akerlof and Janet L. Yellen, "The Fair Wage/Effort Hypothesis and Unemployment," 1988. For more of the same, plus an explicit working-out of the fiscal policy implications of the appearance of wage rates in utility and production functions, see the thoroughly interesting paper by Serge-Christophe Kolm, "Chômage et Politiques Résultant des Rôles de Norme, de Statut ou de Signe des Salaires," in the *Festschrift* for Edmond Malinvaud (Economica, Paris, 1988). The volume will be published in an English edition by MIT Press.

The essay by Clark Kerr appeared in the *American Economic Review* of May 1950. It was reprinted in his *Labor Markets and Wage Determination* (University of California Press, 1977). The passage quoted appears on pages 47–8 of that book. The quotation from Pigors and Myers *Personnel Administration* comes from page 362 of the ninth edition, McGraw-Hill, 1981.

For the Illinois experiment see Bruce D. Meyer, "Implications of the Illinois Reemployment Bonus Experiments for Theories of Unemployment and Policy Design," NBER Working Paper No. 1783, December 1988. For the work–welfare experiments, see "Reforming Welfare with Work" by Judith M. Gueron, Occasional Paper No. 2 of the Ford Foundation Project on Social Welfare and the American Future, 1987; and also "A Survey of Participants and Worksite Supervisors in the New York City Work Experience Program," by Gregory Hoerz and Karla Hanson, MDRC Working Paper, September 1986. Both contain many references to other reports by MDRC.

Marshall's essay is reprinted in *Memorials of Alfred Marshall*, edited by A.C. Pigou (Macmillan, 1925). Passages quoted appear on pages 212, 213, 214, and 217.

On Switzerland, see the paper by J.-P. Danthine and J.-C. Lambelet, "The Swiss Recipe: Conservative Policies Ain't Enough," in *Economic Policy*, October 1987, pages 147–79. The Swiss experience is placed in a longer historical context by Lambelet in "The Swiss Labor Scene, or Why Humans Sometimes Cooperate and Sometimes Don't," Working Paper No. 8808 of the Département d'économétrie et d'économie politique, University of Lausanne, September 1988. Lambelet finds evidence that Austria, West Germany, Japan, The Netherlands and Sweden conform in some degree to the Swiss pattern.

The finding by Blanchflower and Oswald is in

their paper "The Wage Curve," Working Paper No. 1122 of the Centre for Labour Economics at the London School of Economics, dated December 1988. It will eventually appear in a book under the same title. After the Royer Lectures were delivered I discovered "The Employer Size Wage Effect" by Charles Brown and James Medoff, NBER Working Paper No. 2870, March 1989. They present extensive evidence that large firms and large establishments tend to pay higher wages than smaller ones for equivalent jobs. Even after allowing for the possibility that large employers are able to attract higher-quality workers, they find that most of the size effect remains. The authors have no good explanation to offer. The facts are not easily compatible with straightforward supply and demand. They fit more easily with the rent-sharing view proposed in the second lecture; but that is a relatively cheap observation to make.

The observation that interindustrial wage differences are substantial and persistent goes back at least to Sumner Slichter in the 1950s. The question has recently been reexamined by Alan Krueger and Lawrence Summers and by William Dickens and Lawrence Katz. (See "Reflections on the Inter-Industry Wage Structure" and "Inter-Industry Wage Differences and Industry Characteristics," chapters 2 and 3, respectively, in *Unemployment and the Structure of Labor Markets*, edited by K. Lang and J. Leonard (Blackwell, Oxford, 1987), pages 14–47 and 48–89. See also Alan Krueger and Lawrence Summers, "Efficiency Wages and the Inter-Industry

Wage Structure," *Econometrica*, volume 56, number 2 (March 1988), pages 259–93.) With more and better data and more powerful methods, they confirm the basic result. Profitability, establishment size, and capital intensity seem to be industrial correlates of high wages. These regularities are generally supportive of the notion that wages arise as an outcome of bargaining over rents.

In a recent paper, P.-A. Edin and J. Zetterberg of Uppsala University show that similar but much smaller wage differentials exist in Sweden. In view of the adoption by Swedish unions of an explicitly "solidaristic" policy, I take this to confirm the importance of perceived fairness as a force in wage determination.

It is a standard theoretical move in economics to ask: if jobs provide rents and if there are unemployed workers, why do firms not capture the rents for themselves by "selling" the jobs, that is, by requiring some up-front concession from newly hired workers? The absence or infrequency of such devices is then said to cast doubt on the existence of rents. There is an interesting and broadly inclusive discussion of this issue in "Employee Crime and the Monitoring Puzzle" by William Dickens, Lawrence Katz, Kevin Lang and Lawrence Summers, *Journal of Labor Economics*, July 1989. Their conclusion is that rent-extraction devices tend to be ruled out by the unwillingness of courts to enforce them and by social pressures that stigmatize them as unfair exercises of short-side power. As the saying goes, I can live with that.

2 Persistent Unemployment

Persistent unemployment has been a persistent problem for economic theory. It is obviously a problem for the persistently unemployed. They suffer a loss of income, often a deterioration of skills, and sometimes a period of unpleasant uncertainty about the longer future. The problem for the economic theorist is different. What I have been calling textbook economics – the idea that the capitalist economy is a collection of interrelated markets in which supply and demand tend to come into equality – has no good way to explain the fact that fairly high levels of unemployment seem to be able to persist for lengths of time measured in years. A nontrivial part of the history of economics during the past 60 years could be written in terms of the profession's attempts to find a believable story that can account for the facts with minimal damage to the structure of economic theory.

I am not about to recount that history. But I probably have to remind you that an important school of thought in modern economics chooses to deny everything. Its members argue that supply and demand actually do balance in the labor market as

they do in the fish market. Most of the people who are counted as unemployed by the Census are not truly unemployed in the everyday meaning of the word. They are not unable to find work on reasonable terms. Mostly they have chosen not to work now because, given current wage rates and those expected in the future, it is advantageous for them to enjoy leisure now and plan to earn income some time in the future (or to have earned it in the past) when real wage rates will be higher (or were higher) than they are now. There are other versions that have been proposed, some similar to this one, some depending on a different mechanism, but they all tend to agree that the measured unemployed have chosen that status voluntarily. This is not usually a crude bird-dog kennel-dog argument. It does seem to fly in the face of common sense; that may make it attractive to some economists, for the reason that I mentioned at the beginning of these lectures. In fact I do not find this account believable. If it were true, for instance, you would expect sales of goods complementary with leisure – like golf clubs, beachwear, skis and Caribbean cruises – to be higher in recessions when there is a lot of measured unemployment than in prosperous periods when the unemployment rate falls. There is no sign that anything so amusing is true.

Let me make one thing perfectly clear, to quote a famous Keynesian economist. The analysis of a system of well-functioning markets – what we usually call general equilibrium theory – is the main achievement of economics. It is the basic first step

in understanding how a decentralized capitalist economy can work at all. It is the usual point of entry into important practical matters, like the consequences of taxation or the pattern of international trade. The main way that an economist differs from a violinist is the trained habit of tracing how a disturbance to supply or demand in one market ripples through other markets. That achievement is not in question. No doubt it could be improved, just as your favorite violinist's technique could be improved. My argument is that it urgently needs improvement in its treatment of the labor market, because otherwise it forfeits its ability to deal coherently with some socially important events, like prolonged unemployment.

There is no inherent reason why economic theory should not seek slightly offbeat analyses of persistent unemployment. The labor market might just be different in important ways from the market for fish. I spent an hour offering bits and pieces of evidence pointing in that direction in my first lecture. Civilians will take that possibility as a matter of course. I want to emphasize to economists that it is not a betrayal of the structure of economic theory generally to admit the likelihood that labor is a peculiar sort of commodity and the labor market correspondingly a peculiar sort of market.

I grant that it might be especially beautiful – even though a little dull – if all of economics could be summed up in the statement that supply equals demand everywhere nearly all the time, where supply and demand for each commodity come from

the maximization by relevant agents of conventional utility functions subject only to the conventional constraints. But chemists seem to be able to get pleasure from the discovery of materials with anomalous properties and biologists are neither surprised nor dismayed to learn that evolution has produced some very peculiar organisms. And even if chemists and biologists – not to mention historians – were as eager for simplicity and generality as particle physicists seem to be, economists might still prefer to trade some simplicity for a better shot at fitting the facts.

Needless to say, that is exactly what has happened on a partial scale. Some economists have already proposed plausible models of the labor market that are capable of accounting in a logical way for the existence and persistence of true unemployment. The more interesting of these, unsurprisingly, seem to be based on a somewhat more sophisticated view of the labor market as a social institution. They allow for a variety of motives and interactions that are conspicuously missing from the standard textbook model.

The leading candidates these days are versions of what are called, in one case, efficiency–wage theory and, in the other, insider–outsider theory. Lectures like these are not the appropriate vehicle for a full exposition; but I have to say something about them to give you an idea of how they work. For one thing, you will have to judge whether the mechanisms they rely on are reasonable interpretations of the reality of labor markets. And secondly I want to

add something to them. Both, it seems to me, leave the same gap and are vulnerable to the same criticism; I want to propose a way to complete them.

There are many versions of efficiency–wage theory. They all turn one way or another on the observation that workers employed in modern industry often have some control over their own productivity. They produce more when they are strongly motivated to do so. One way for an employer to provide more motivation is by paying more than other employers do; another is to threaten to fire the excessively unproductive if and when they are detected. It all sounds quite natural, but already we have made a significant break with textbook doctrine: if what I just said is true, actual production depends not only on physical inputs and technology, but also on the wage being paid.

From this point on, alternative versions of efficiency–wage theory proceed to emphasize different facts of life. One of the earliest combines the stick with the carrot: workers also provide effort because being found out and fired for cause is costly. It is more costly the harder it is to find another job, and therefore the higher the current unemployment rate happens to be. Even if each employer finds the carrot initially more efficient than the stick (because detection is costly) and tries to pay more than the others, competition among employers will merely bid up wages with no employer being able to establish a lasting favorable differential. In the end the wage will be driven to levels at which full employment is not viable; all the discipline is, in

effect, done by the stick, the threat of unemployment. If there were less unemployment it would pay employers to offer higher wages in the hope of eliciting more productivity from their workers. All would do so; but then with jobs more easily found, and paying more to boot, it would become advantageous for workers to provide less effort and accept the higher risk of being laid off.

There are other styles of efficiency–wage theory. George Akerlof and Janet Yellen have proposed – on the basis of psychological and sociological evidence – what they call the fair-wage–effort hypothesis. In this kinder and gentler version it is not the fear of unemployment and deprivation of wage income that makes individual productivity an increasing function of the wage received, but rather a sort of ethical imperative: if you are paid a fair day's wage you owe your employer a fair day's work. An employer who pays less than a fair day's wage cannot expect to get a fair day's work. It then takes a little analytical machinery to show that a likely outcome is persistent unemployment. (Anyone who wants to go into that can consult the literature.)

I hope all of this strikes you as plausible, even homespun. You could not make it exciting enough for a short story, not even in the *New Yorker*. But there is a general economic insight hidden in this commonplace description. One important difference between the labor market and the market for fish is that the performance of the worker depends on the price paid for her services. You would not say the same for the performance of a pound of filleted

salmon. (By the way, if it should happen that consumers of fish come to judge quality by price – so that salmon tastes better the more you pay for it, *just because* you pay more for it – then the market for fish will begin to behave unclassically too.) Because the wage rate enters the story in this double role, as a productive factor as well as a simple cost, it is not available *simply* to balance supply and demand in the usual efficient way. It cannot perform both functions perfectly. It is precisely the character of the labor market as a social institution that makes it generate an inefficiently low level of employment. That is all I want from efficiency–wage theory right now.

The insider–outsider approach starts from a different elementary observation. The group of experienced workers in a firm – the insiders, for short – is likely not to be perfectly interchangeable with other workers – unemployed workers, for instance – who are currently available in the labor market. The economist would say that the insiders generate a rent jointly with the rest of the apparatus of the firm. They are therefore in a position to bargain with the firm over the division of the rent. The rent may arise initially simply because the insiders are more productive in this firm than outsiders would be. It will be enlarged if the insiders can jointly threaten to resist the hiring of outsiders by refusing to train them or to cooperate with them. That may require a certain amount of solidarity. In any case, the insiders can hope to achieve a wage higher than the level that would allow the firm profitably

to employ any number of unemployed workers, assuming there are some.

If that is the way the labor market works, then pretty clearly unemployment can persist. Wages are too high for full employment, and the intrinsic advantage and bargaining power enjoyed by insiders is adequate to keep those wages from being eroded by the competition of the unemployed. I will let you make the contrast with the fish market yourself.

These stories connect up with the textbook model in an interesting way. The reason why the textbook model has such a hard time accommodating persistent unemployment is that unemployed workers are supposed to put downward pressure on wage rates by competing for existing jobs. Economists would put that in a more precise and general way. To say that there is true or involuntary unemployment is to say that those without jobs would regard themselves as better off if they were employed in jobs they know how to do at the wages now being paid to those roughly equivalent workers who hold such jobs. In that case (if individuals care only about the goods they consume and the leisure they enjoy) they would feel themselves to be better off if they were employed in jobs they can do even if they were paid ever so slightly less than the going wage in such jobs. If one means by an equilibrium a situation in which no participant can think of anything more advantageous to do than he is now doing, this situation with involuntary unemployment cannot be an equilibrium. Unemployed workers could bid for jobs. In the sort of labor market that underlies the

textbook, they should do so.

Both of the novel labor-market stories I have described explain why *employers* would reject competitive offers from the unemployed. The reasons are different in the two models, of course. In the efficiency–wage story, the employer reasons this way. I am offering the wage that I now pay because it is the best wage for me to offer when I take account of its effect on productivity. No doubt the currently unemployed are sincere when they offer to work for a few cents less. But I know that if I were to hire them after a slight wage cut to replace some of my current workers, the newcomers would pretty soon supply less than the optimal amount of effort – less than optimal *for me*, mind you – either because they would have less than the optimal fear of being found out and laid off or because they would feel aggrieved at getting less than a fair wage. Maybe their instant feeling of relief or gratitude at having found a job would deter them for a while. But it would wear off. They are, after all, exactly like their currently employed sisters-in-law, by definition. And that is how I arrived at the going wage in the first place. No, thank you, it is not to my advantage to pay less.

In the insider–outsider case the reason is different but the reality is the same. If I accept any of these wage-cutting offers, I will disturb the balance I have reached with my current insiders. They will very likely make life hard for any small number of outsiders, especially as the insiders will blame the outsiders for the erosion of the wage. The

productivity of the enterprise will suffer. If I were to try a wholesale replacement of insiders by outsiders, the loss of firm-specific skills will probably cost me more in profit than a lower wage would bring. Besides, I would merely be replacing my current insiders by a group who would soon become the insiders of the future. And then they would act exactly like their sisters-in-law, by definition. No, thank you, it is not to my advantage to pay less.

This is a powerful result. It resolves an important paradox. When there are a lot of unemployed workers, you might expect employers actively to solicit competitive wage cutting on their part. It rarely happens. The cases when it does happen, usually in deep recession or when there is a serious threat from imported substitutes for the firm's product, are striking enough to call attention to the fact that it does not happen in run-of-the-mill recessions, although the unemployment rate might rise by two or three percentage points and even in average times there appears to be some excess supply of labor. The alternative theories I have sketched at least explain why employers might not try to induce wage cutting and might not accept offers if they came along anyway.

But these stories seem to be incomplete. They do not explain why the unemployed do not at least try to compete for existing jobs by offering to work at less than the going wage. One possible explanation is that they know from hearsay or experience that such offers would be turned down by potential employers. There is undoubtedly something to that.

The collective experience of the labor market (as even relative newcomers must learn) would say that. It would be reinforced by the fact that, in bad times, firms normally let it be known that they are not hiring. Nevertheless, this explanation seems a little lame. It costs very little to try; and the potential gain to any unemployed worker who succeeded would be substantial. There would seem to be some deeper force at work to choke off wage competition from the unemployed. Even in the years of deep recession and import competition, when wage give-backs occurred with some frequency, they were generally initiated by employers, not by competition from the unemployed. The threat was usually to close down a plant, not so often to staff it with unemployed workers. In some European countries, where unemployment rates have been very high by historical standards for an unprecedentedly long time, there has been no tendency for real wages to erode; in fact in some countries they appear to continue rising. One would feel better with a model that explained this apparent unwillingness of unemployed labor to bid actively for scarce jobs. For economists, quite a lot turns on this point. In the absence of any such theory, the temptation is strong to accept the view that measured unemployment is "voluntary" in the sense that the "unemployed" are not worse off than their employed sisters-in-law.

One easy way out of this difficulty is the hypothesis that there is some sort of social norm or behavioral injunction that forbids undercutting the going wage

as a strategy for unemployed workers. The hypothesis has the advantage that it feels true, precisely because a job is a status as well as a source of income. It does not require any romanticism about solidarity to suggest that competing for an existing job by undercutting the wage might be seen as demeaning, whereas selling off your full load of halibut at the market-clearing price, whatever it may be, would carry no corresponding overtone of betrayal or self-abnegation. The fact that the norm against wage cutting seems to break down in extreme circumstances may only testify to its reality in run-of-the-mill cases. We sense that something has snapped.

I confess that I believe the right answer lies in this direction. But that is hardly an adequate argument. The casual postulation of social norms is altogether too easy a mode of explanation. It will certainly not do for economists, including me, partly because we like to think of ourselves as more hard-boiled than that and partly because we are professionally inclined to think of self-interest as a powerful motive in economic affairs.

An injunction not to engage in wage cutting puts a major strain on unemployed workers. The cost of obeying the norm is undoubtedly diminished by the availability of unemployment insurance and other public assistance benefits. These differ in amount from time to time and place to place. At most times and in most places, the margin of advantage of employment over unemployment remains pretty substantial. Besides, there is plenty of evidence –

some of which I described in the first lecture – that
a job is a source of self-respect in a way that even
moderately cushy unemployment could never be.
You have to be pretty obtuse not to realize that
very many of the unemployed would much prefer
to be working at wage rates currently on offer.
Presumably that is why they and their families have
been known to celebrate the acquisition of a job.
("Write if you get work.") But then the belief that
there is a stable and effective social norm against
wage competition for jobs needs some reinforcement
of a kind that might come from a showing that
obeying such a norm is individually rational, besides
performing a social function. That is the sort of
argument I now want to make in a non-technical
way.

I begin with a general sort of framework and
come down to my particular problem later. Probably
everyone here knows about the prisoner's dilemma
game which, in recent years, has provided a neat
vehicle for the study of a whole range of social
interactions. We can do without the circumstantial
story-line that usually brightens up the description
of the situation. The essence of the game is that
there are two players, A and B, each of whom must
choose one of two possible strategies without any
possibility of preliminary communication and certainly without the capacity to make binding commit-
ments about which strategy each will choose. The
two strategies available to each player are called
Cooperation and Defection, for reasons which

emerge from the nature of the game. Each combination of choices, one for each player, leads to a known payoff to each. The particular payoffs have a key property: no matter whether A cooperates or defects, it is to B's advantage to defect; and no matter whether B cooperates or defects, it is to A's advantage to defect. We have to suppose then that both A and B will defect, certainly if they have no particular connection with one another except through a single play of this game. However, if both do defect, the payoff to each of them is perceptibly less than it would have been if both had cooperated. It is individually rational for each player to defect, although each of them knows that it would be jointly and individually better if they were both to cooperate. If they could negotiate a binding agreement beforehand, they would surely agree to cooperate.

There is not much more to say if the players are healthily self-interested and play the game only once. The plot thickens if they have to play the game again and again, for a very long time, even if they remain quite selfish. Then it would be driven home to the players that it would be worth a lot if they could find a way to cooperate effectively. The besetting obstacle to cooperation is the reasonable fear that the other will play you for a sucker and let you cooperate while he or she defects. If the game is played many times, however, there is a possible escape from mutual assured defection. Each player may be able to teach the other, by example

and experience if necessary, that each is prepared to punish defection by the other. If A should ever take advantage of B by defecting while B cooperates, B can respond by herself defecting for a whole string of plays. This is costly to B, but the cost may be more than recovered if A is taught a lasting lesson. A may come to realize that the short-run gain from suckering B does not compensate for the long-run loss from a string of mutual defections that might have been mutual cooperations.

(If cooperation is to emerge in this way, it is obviously essential that the game be played more or less forever. There is a well-known problem in the finitely repeated game: the last play is just one-shot; but then the next-to-last play is also effectively one-shot because the last play is bound to result in defection; and thus the whole thing unravels. When we are talking about social phenomena this difficulty is not so acute. Individual players may come and go, but the game – wage bargaining, for example – goes on effectively forever and institutional memory can take over. Alternatively one can make do with a probability that the game will be played at least one more time.)

All this is old stuff and has been much discussed and analyzed by game theorists and others. The political scientist Robert Axelrod has written a well-known book called *The Evolution of Cooperation*, whose subject is well described by its title. Axelrod shows by example that the simplest punishment strategy, which he calls Tit for Tat, does very well in repeated plays of the game against other

reasonable strategies. (Tit for Tat starts by cooperat-
ing on the first play and then on each succeeding
play does whatever its opponent did on the play
before. Thus cooperation is rewarded by cooperation
and defection is punished by a single defection.) It
does not require a vast leap of imagination to see
how the habit of cooperation might emerge and be
reinforced.

But then the next step could very well be the
acceptance and internalization of a social norm:
cooperation is the right thing to do in such and such
a particular social situation. It is a fair guess that
many social norms evolve in just this manner, not
merely from prisoner's dilemma contexts. Behavior
that has been found to be individually tempting but
socially destructive is held to be socially unacceptable. Behavior that has been found to be collectively
useful though at least mildly disadvantageous to the
individual is held to be the right thing to do. Some
conflict between the private and social consequences
of actions seems to be a necessary part of the
picture, for otherwise there is no need for a specific
code of behavior. Too much conflict, on the other
hand, could cause a cooperative norm to break
down. The last step is the internalization of social
norms: we do things because they are the right thing
to do, not because we have reckoned all the
consequences.

To come back to the labor market, I have
something more specific in mind than these rather
vague thoughts arising from the prisoner's dilemma.
But some of the concepts, like that of a punishment

strategy, will play a further role. The problem, remember, is to explain how it can be that unemployed workers do not compete for jobs by offering to work for less than incumbents are getting, although it would appear to be to their advantage to do just that. The solution I want to propose goes as follows. The labor-market outcome is best thought of as a single episode in a repeated game involving firms and workers. In any single episode, some workers are employed and others are unemployed. Being unemployed but sitting tight and accepting the loss that comes with unemployment can be an "equilibrium strategy" for an unemployed worker. That means that there is an assignment of behavior patterns to each player such that, in the repeated game context, no player can gain from adopting a different strategy if the others stand pat. In such an equilibrium, the behavior pattern assigned to the unemployed worker is the one I have described, and the one we by and large observe.

This idea seems to have occurred simultaneously to Jörgen Weibull, a young Swedish economist, and to Frank Hahn and me working collaboratively. I will not try to fill in the details here, but just focus on the principle. It will sound terribly abstract, but that may be appropriate, since all I am after is the principle; in any case it is typical of economic theory.

Imagine a single firm that has attached to it a pool of identical workers. The workers have a common "reservation wage." That is, there is a wage rate so low that people would be indifferent between working at that wage and not having a job at all.

If, for instance, there is a standard level of public assistance available to any unemployed worker, then the reservation wage might be a little below that (if having a job makes people feel good) or a bit above that (if working is merely irksome). Now suppose that, even if the market wage rate equals the reservation wage, the firm would not be willing to employ everyone in the labor pool. This is just to guarantee that there will be some unemployment; remember I am not trying to explain how unemployment comes about, but only how it can persist. Then at any wage higher than the reservation wage there will be involuntary unemployment; those with jobs are better off than those without. At the reservation wage there is unemployment but, according to the definition, it is voluntary. The wage cannot go below the reservation wage, because no one would then want a job. For one reason or another, workers do not form a union. The atomistic case is the key case anyway.

The textbook story about this isolated labor market is utterly simple. The only possible market wage is the reservation wage. Any higher wage rate would be competed down by involuntarily unemployed workers. No one would show up at any lower wage. (In our jargon: at any higher wage the supply of labor would be the whole labor force, so there would be excess supply; at any lower wage the supply of labor would be zero, so there would be excess demand.) At the reservation wage, the firm would employ as many workers as it finds profitable. The rest would go on the dole; but they

would be no worse off than the employed, all things considered.

Now suppose instead that the firm and the workers play an indefinitely repeated game in the same artificial setting. The rules of the game allow the firm to quote a single wage rate. Each worker then decides whether he or she would be willing to work at that wage, and so signifies. The firm then hires as many among them as it wishes, presumably the number that gives the firm the largest profit it can get. If there are fewer jobs than willing workers, the firm fills the jobs at random from the pool of willing workers. The rest go on the dole; but now they are involuntarily unemployed, provided the quoted wage is higher than the reservation wage.

The fundamental question is: can such a state of affairs be stable, repeating itself period after period, with the wage higher than the reservation wage and accompanying persistent unemployment? Well, it can. To see that it can, we need to specify an "equilibrium strategy" for the firm and for each worker.

For the firm the strategy in question is simple. Offer the equilibrium wage, whatever it is, every period, as long as no worker ever offers to work for less. If anyone ever undercuts, offer the reservation wage forever after. For the workers – who are all alike – the equilibrium strategy is almost as simple. Offer to work at the going wage. If you end up unemployed, live on the dole for that period. But if anyone ever works for less than the going wage, offer to work at the reservation wage forever after.

(The "forever" is overly strong, but never mind.)

The key is the threatened reversion to Hobbesian competition if the proposed equilibrium ever breaks down. That is a sort of punishment strategy and serves the purpose of enforcing the equilibrium with persistent unemployment without wage cutting. To verify that these are equilibrium strategies, one has to show that it pays no party to deviate from them. The firm has no reason to deviate: if no one has offered to undercut the wage up to now, then no one will accept a wage reduction. The first must either go along or go out of business. Now suppose you are an unemployed worker in some period. Should you offer to work for less than the going wage? You calculate the consequences. This period you will be better off and your gain is measured by the difference between the wage you actually get and the reservation wage which is what you get on the dole. Forever after, however, you and everyone else are doomed to the reservation wage, because the punishment strategy will be invoked. Now suppose you do not undercut. This period you get the reservation wage. For the future you take your chances and you get the present discounted value of an income stream that consists of the reservation wage when you are unemployed and the market wage when you are employed. You will undercut if the first prospect is better than the second; you will sit tight if the second prospect is better than the first.

Which will it be? Well, you will undercut if you care hardly at all or not at all about the future. The

prospect of Hobbesian competition in the future will not scare you and the prospect of a reasonable income stream in the future will not please you. But the less you discount the future, the more likely you will be to sit tight. Similarly, if the unemployment rate is very high you may be inclined to defect, because if you do not you will be unemployed most of the time in the future anyway, so Hobbesian competition is no great threat. If the unemployment rate is low, you would be foolish to sacrifice a long stream of probable employment at market wages for a single immediate gain. Actually, in this model, the unemployment rate depends on the going wage, because the firm will hire more people the lower the wage happens to be. The result I am after can be stated in the following way. For any given rate of discounting the future, there is a range – an interval – of wage rates any one of which can be an equilibrium market wage for this game, with accompanying persistent unemployment. The higher the wage, the more unemployment there will be. Within that range there will be no undercutting on the part of the unemployed, because the reversion to Hobbesian competition will be unfavorable for everyone, including them.

It goes without saying, I hope, that this game is intended as an extended metaphor, not a literal description. Nobody adopts a formal strategy or calculates the consequences of all possible deviations from it, or knows what strategy others have adopted. What actually happens is altogether different. I presume that experience and reason lead to the

emergence of a social norm. We do not compete for each other's jobs by nibbling away at wage levels because we have been taught that it is unfair to do so, or demeaning, or unacceptable, or – perhaps – self-destructive. I suppose a reflective person might rationalize that sort of norm with the perception that life in the labor market would be very unpleasant – nasty, brutish and short, you might say – without it. I do not know how such norms get established, historically speaking, but once established they draw their force from shared values and social approbation and disapprobation, not from calculation. Eventually they become internalized. Most soldiers, when captured, give just their name, rank, and serial number.

This process, however it works, is an integral part of the story. As students of infinitely repeated games know, the no-undercutting equilibrium that I have exhibited is only one of many such equilibria of the same game, some of which will look very different. (Indeed, perpetual Hobbesian competition, leading to the textbook solution, is another.) So the fact that the no-undercutting equilibrium exists is no argument that it will be reached or ever observed. The implication goes in the opposite direction. We observe situations with persistent unemployment and without wage competition. The game story rationalizes that fact; and the hypothesis about the formation and reinforcement of behavioral norms helps to explain how this rationalization might be sustained. If the shoe fits, we can wear it.

What I have tried to do in this lecture is to sketch

the sort of model of the labor market that might serve as an alternative to the textbook model. It is a better model, both because it rings truer as a description of the life we lead and see others lead, and because it can make room for important phenomena like persistent unemployment and sticky wages that embarrass the simple supply-and-demand model. I do not feel confident enough about the precise form of the alternative to want to insist on any particular version. It will be enough for my purposes to draw some general conclusions: that an economy like ours can be at rest with a range of unemployment rates and/or wage levels, that persistent unemployment need not be voluntary or "efficient," and that there is at least an opportunity for policy to improve the state of the economy.

In the next lecture I want to say something about the implications for policy that arise from this view of the labor market as a social institution. I would not dream of promoting concrete policy measures on the basis of such general ideas as I have tried to convey. I did not come all the way from Cambridge to Berkeley to tell you that education and training are good things, for instance. But it can do no harm to ask the general question whether there are valid approaches to employment policy that tend to get ruled out of court unjustly by the textbook model of the labor market. The answer will be that there are.

Bibliographical Note

The best way to get better acquainted with efficiency–wage theory is the compendium of republished articles collected in *Efficiency Wage Models of the Labor Market* (Cambridge University Press, 1986) edited by George Akerlof and Janet Yellen, who add an enlightening introduction. This volume includes the paper by Carl Shapiro and Joseph Stiglitz that is most often cited in connection with the detection-of-shirking version of the theory. I confess to lingering doubts about this version. Detection does not seem all that hard and the costs of detection seem pretty small. A large dog is being wagged by a mighty small tail. I am encouraged to mention these casual doubts because I am relieved to notice that they are shared by Lloyd Ulman: see his preliminary working paper "Labor Market Analysis and Concerted Behavior," Institute of Industrial Relations, Berkeley, January 1989. For the Akerlof–Yellen Fair Wage/Effort Hypothesis see their paper "The Fair Wage/Effort Hypothesis and Unemployment," 1988.

The insider–outsider model is developed in a series of papers by Assar Lindbeck and Dennis Snower. An easily accessible one is "Cooperation, Harassment, and Involuntary Unemployment," *American Economic Review*, March 1988, pages 167–88. A full account of their work has been published by MIT Press under the title *The Insider–Outsider Theory of Employment and Unemployment* (1988). See also

Olivier Blanchard and Lawrence Summers, "Hysteresis and the European Unemployment Problem," in *NBER Macroeconomics Annual* (MIT Press, 1986), pages 15–78.

There is a large technical literature on the repeated prisoner's dilemma. One place to start is chapter 9 of Martin Shubik's *Game Theory in the Social Sciences* (MIT Press, 1983). For my purposes Axelrod's *The Evolution of Cooperation* (Basic Books, 1984) has the advantage of focusing on how the habit of cooperation might come about. See also Michael Taylor, *The Possibility of Cooperation* (Cambridge University Press, 1988). The book by Edna Ullmann–Margalit, *The Emergence of Norms* (Oxford, 1977) seems to me not quite to clinch its case. There is an excellent but, as far as I know, unpublished paper by Michael C. Blad (University of Sydney) and Nicholas Oulton (University of Lancaster), "Union–Firm Bargaining as a Repeated Prisoner's Dilemma," dated September 1986; it makes explicit use of a bargaining framework.

The paper by Jörgen Weibull is "Persistent Unemployment as Subgame Perfect Equilibrium," Seminar Paper No. 381 of the Institute for International Economic Studies, Stockholm, May 1987. As mentioned, Frank Hahn and I have developed the same idea at the same time; it will appear as part of a book in progress. Yet another example, just discovered, is S.R. Osmani, "Wage Determination in Rural Labour Markets: The Theory of Implicit Cooperation," WIDER Working Paper, December 1988.

Appendix

Even at this late date, it might be a good idea to give an example of a prisoner's dilemma game. Player A chooses a row and player B chooses a column, each in ignorance of the other's choice. Choice C corresponds to Cooperation, D to Defection. Each box of the table reports the payoff to the players, A's in the lower left corner, B's in the upper right. Whatever choice B makes, A is better off defecting, because 9 is bigger than 8 and 4 is bigger than 3. Similarly, whatever choice A makes, B is better off defecting, as the payoff table shows. If the game is played once without any opportunity for effective coordination, both players will defect. The payoffs will be 4 to A and 5 to B. Both would be better off if both cooperated: the payoffs would be 8 to A and 9 to B. Both players know that, but neither can afford to cooperate; if the other player defects, the cooperator is worse off yet. The lecture describes how this outcome might be avoided in a repeated-game context.

In the lecture it is argued that the availability of punishment strategies makes it possible that wage rigidity can be an equilibrium outcome even in the face of involuntary unemployment. Now I want to provide a little more detail.

All workers in the firm's labor pool are alike. The reservation wage is w_0 in every period and every worker has the discount factor $d < 1$. Can a constant wage $w > w_0$ be an equilibrium? (In all this, nothing

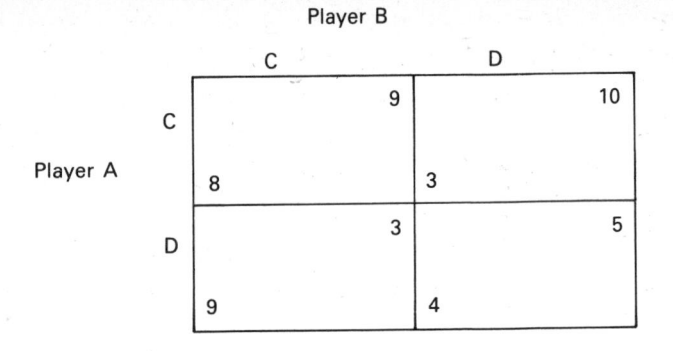

changes if w and w_0 are the utilities associated with employment at the market wage and with unemployment at the reservation wage.) Let $e = e(w)$ be the fraction of the labor pool that the firm chooses to employ when the wage is w. The assumptions made in the lecture ensure that $e(w) < e(w_0) < 1$. The unemployment rate is $1 - e = u$. Jobs are allocated to workers at random, independently in each period.

Now suppose that the market wage is w and you learn that you will be unemployed this period. You must decide whether to undercut the market wage or to sit tight and accept w_0. We can suppose harmlessly that you can undercut by an arbitrarily small amount, so that you will receive (almost) w this period. But if you do, you know that for the next T periods the reservation wage will prevail. This option has present value $w + w_0 (d + d^2 + \ldots + d^T) = w + w_0 d(1 - d^T)/(1 - d) = w + kw_0$.

If you sit tight this period, you get w_0. Then, supposing everyone behaves similarly, you will have your fair chance of a job at wage w in each of the

next T periods and so your expected outcome will be $ew + (1 - e)w_0$ each time. The present value of this option is $w_0 + k[ew + (1 - e)w_0]$. We can take it that the still later history is the same for both options and thus does not affect your choice.

The second option is better than the first if

$$w_0 + k[ew + (1 - e)w_0] > w + kw_0$$

and in that case neither you nor any other worker will wish to deviate on the assumption that no one else does. Arithmetic shows that this inequality reduces to

$$(w - w_0)(1 - ke) < 0.$$

Since $w > w_0$, not undercutting is an equilibrium strategy if and only if $e(w) > 1/k$ or $u(w) < 1 - 1/k$.

The firm's demand for labor from its pool is a decreasing function of w, so $u(w)$ is an increasing function of w. The figure is a plot of $u(w)$ against w. By assumption, $u(w_0) > 0$. Let w_1 solve $u(w) = 1 - 1/k$. The diagram shows that a no-undercutting equilibrium is possible as long as $w_0 < w < w_1$. Since $k = d + d^2 + \ldots + d^T$, it increases with both d and T. So does $1 - 1/k$. Thus, as expected, a longer punishment period enlarges the set of equilibrium wage rates and a higher discount factor – more care about the future – does the same. (See p. 56 for the diagram.)

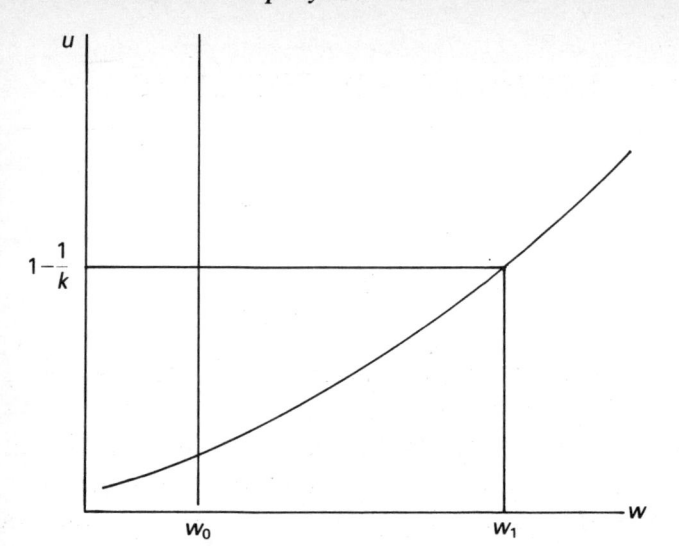

3   Implications for Practice

The distinguishing characteristic of crazy people is that they keep telling anyone who will listen that they are not crazy. In that same serious spirit I want to remind you that there is method in my madness. In the first lecture, I tried generally to undermine the notion – almost a reflex reaction among economists – that the operation of the labor market can be summed up by the simple formula that the (real or nominal) wage tries to equalize supply and demand, so that the only meaningful equilibrium situation is one in which there is neither excess supply nor excess demand. My argument was that all our experience teaches us that the motives governing behavior in the labor market are not exactly the same as those that govern the market when a fleet of fishing vessels returns to port and auctions off its combined catch at dockside. Given that the motives are different and more complex, it is to be expected that labor-market institutions will evolve in a way that does not simply mimic those we usually suppose to characterize a Walrasian economy.

One of the advantages of family life is that my wife, in reading a draft of that lecture, was able to

remind me that she had come to similar conclusions when studying the market for long-term tenancy agreements in nineteenth-century Irish agriculture. That is not surprising, when you come to think of it. In agricultural communities, the occupation of land is likely to be encrusted with as many and as intense non-Walrasian characteristics as the occupation of a job in industrial communities.

In the second lecture, I tried to show you that such motives and attitudes lend themselves to equilibrium concepts other than price-mediated market clearing of the conventional kind. There is equilibrium in the labor market when none of the participants is willing to choose, from among the eligible strategies, something other than the strategy currently being pursued. The nature of equilibrium therefore depends a lot on the common perception of the set of eligible strategies. That is one way in which the particular status of the labor market can infiltrate itself into economic theory. Any definition of equilibrium needs support from a description of out-of-equilibrium behavior; so there is no avoiding a specification of goals and strategies.

Once this is recognized and taken seriously, there are almost too many special characteristics of the labor market begging to be incorporated in a descriptive theory of the determination of wage rates and employment. I found it necessary to go only a little beyond ideas that have been in circulation for a while.

One common consequence of these theoretical extensions is especially noteworthy. There can be

many equilibrium configurations for a labor market, many situations in which no significant number of participants feels driven to change their behavior. There may be a range of levels of employment and wage rates that can persist as part of an equilibrium configuration even if there is a unique level of employment associated with each wage rate. This is unlike our usual view of a single market where supply and demand curves have nonzero and opposite slopes. The more institutional point of view suggests that the labor market can be in equilibrium with any one of a range of unemployment rates. That does not mean *any* unemployment rate: the range of possible equilibrium unemployment rates can be limited above and below.

This idea entails another: if there is a range of equilibrium unemployment rates, then the one we actually observe depends on history and not only on structural characteristics of the labor market. I do not mean this in any deep sense, in which institutions themselves are to be regarded as the outcome of a particular evolution. That is undoubtedly so, but there is no need to go that far. What matters is that, if the labor market could be at rest with any one of several unemployment rates, maybe even a whole interval of unemployment rates, then the accident of history may be the decisive factor in deciding which of them is reached at any particular time.

Now I want to carry that train of thought a step further. If there is a range of equilibrium unemployment rates then the scope for economic

policy is automatically broadened. There are probably always policy actions that can affect the equilibrium unemployment rate by altering the structural fundamentals of the labor market. Even the most conventional theory of the labor market allows that possibility; one difference is that we are now considering an extended set of fundamental characteristics. Beyond that, however, economic policy may be able to move the labor market from one possible equilibrium configuration to another. There is a sense in which policy can create artificial initial conditions, an alternative history almost, and thus alter the equilibrium configuration without really needing to cause a change in tastes or technology or anything nearly as drastic as that.

I want to do two things in this lecture. The first is to cite some empirical evidence that seems to lend credibility to the idea that the labor market can have many equilibrium configurations. I want to stipulate at the beginning that the evidence I have in mind is only suggestive and not at all conclusive. All I think it says, at this stage, is that the oddball picture of the labor market has about as much going for it as the standard view. Or perhaps I should put it the other way: that the currently orthodox view of the labor market rests on rather weak evidence and ought to be viewed with healthy skepticism. Common sense has as much evidence on its side as the artful textbook theory has on its side. (This may be a tactical error on my part; maybe the only way to make converts is to adopt an air of certainty.

That would be too bad. I am not good at adopting an air of certainty.)

My second goal in this lecture is to speculate a little about the course economic policy might follow in this alternative sort of world. Suppose the objective were to put an end to persistent unemployment at the levels that have ruled until very recently in Great Britain, West Germany and France, where unemployment for the past 8 to 9 years has been consistently higher than 8–9 percent of the labor force. Suppose the target were to achieve a situation more like Sweden or Norway, where unemployment rates have been running at 2–3 percent, or like Switzerland with unemployment at 1 percent or even less. What might one think of doing?

Here too I want to walk carefully. It leaps to the eye that the low-unemployment countries I have mentioned are all small and socially homogeneous societies, whereas the high-unemployment countries are large, diverse, less cohesive societies, harder to manage, less likely – perhaps – to be able to work out a coordinated, norm-guided, cooperative solution to the prisoner's dilemma aspects of the labor market. Where the United States fits in the scheme of things I leave to observers more acute and thinkers more deep than I.

I am not going to produce a full menu of policy initiatives aimed at improving the condition of the labor market in Europe and North America. Any sensible prescription would have to pay attention to the local peculiarities of individual countries, the

state of the goods markets, and no doubt to many other things. All I am really looking for are some ideas about labor-market policy that might flow logically from the picture of the labor market itself that I have been advocating. Even so, I fear that there will be several commonplaces for every new thought.

The 1980s have been years of high and persistent unemployment in the large European economies. Between 1970 and 1975 the unemployment rates averaged about 3 percent in France, about 1 percent in Germany and about 4 percent in Great Britain. Between 1981 and 1988 the corresponding figures were 9–10 percent in France, 8–9 percent in Germany and 10–11 percent in Great Britain. Nor have I just picked out extreme years in widely fluctuating series. The truth is that there was not so much variation in the late 1960s and early 1970s, just routine fluctuations around a low average, and not much variation in the 1980s, just routine fluctuations around a high average. Between 1975 and 1981 unemployment rates rose pretty steadily.

The contemporary version of textbook economics has a special way of accounting for this dramatic change in the functioning of the labor market (and the rest of the economy). There is at any instant a (presumably well-defined though perhaps not easily knowable) equilibrium unemployment rate. I shall call it that for now, though the terminology and the background story can vary a lot from textbook to textbook. The defining property of the equilibrium

unemployment rate is that a lower unemployment rate, maintained for any length of time, would necessarily lead to accelerating inflation; and a higher unemployment rate, maintained for any length of time, would lead to accelerating deflation. That is not quite the same thing as the unemployment rate that makes the demand for labor equal to the supply of labor. Some of the accompanying stories do have distinct market-clearing overtones, however, and none that I know of is very far from that interpretation.

If, then, unemployment is persistently higher in the 1980s than the years earlier, it can only mean that the equilibrium unemployment rate in the large European countries was around 3 percent in the 1970s and around 9 percent during most of the 1980s. After all, inflation is neither accelerating drastically nor decelerating drastically in any of those countries as would have to be the case if their labor markets were not in equilibrium in the relevant sense. In fact, it is possible to offer some reasons why the equilibrium unemployment rate might have risen: excessive regulatory and other obstacles to labor mobility, legal restrictions on the ability of firms to discharge unneeded workers (which leads them to be hesitant about hiring in the first place), excessively high real wage rates enforced by trade unions equipped with escalator clauses, generous social insurance and unemployment compensation benefits that reduce the effective supply of labor, etc. I have no doubt that some, maybe all, of these things are true in some degree; but I have the strong

impression that Robert J. Gordon has exploded the coherence of this story by showing that it will not work in detail: real wages moving in the wrong direction, unemployment insurance benefits becoming less generous, and so on. (I will refer to Gordon's work again in another context.)

A more favorable case can be made for this theory in the United States. Here, for instance, the extraordinarily high unemployment of 1982 and 1983 did actually bring about disinflation; and our unemployment rates have in fact come down. No convenient *ex post facto* juggling with equilibrium unemployment rates appears to be necessary, though the American discussion has not been free of that either.

The key empirical claim in this literature is the "accelerationist" property: there is only a single unemployment rate that is compatible with a stable rate of inflation for any substantial length of time. The interpretation of that critical unemployment rate as representing the clearing of the labor market is only an interpretation – the most popular one but not the only one possible. For this to be a meaningful doctrine, it is important that the critical unemployment rate should be a slowly changing "structural" characteristic of the labor market and not some casual or erratic will o'the wisp.

Some years ago Franco Modigliani and Lucas Papademos suggested a simple and direct way of testing the accelerationist theory. They looked at year-to-year changes in the rate of wage inflation and compared them with the current or just-past

unemployment rates. Accelerationism says that the acceleration should be faster the lower the unemployment rate; and the equilibrium or "natural" unemployment rate can be estimated as the unemployment rate at which the acceleration is just about zero.

In December 1987 Professor Donald Nichols of the University of Wisconsin returned to this straightforward device and used it to survey American experience for the past 30 years or so. He found, with a minimum of jiggery-pokery, that there did appear to be such a relation between wage acceleration and the unemployment rate. Moreover one could defensibly conclude that the "natural" rate, at which acceleration passes through zero, is somewhere around $5\frac{1}{2}$ percent, or maybe a fraction less, and had been there for some 30 years. There seemed to be no particular need to hypothesize any trend or other perceptible change in the natural rate. One would have to say that experience in the 2 years after Nichols's period seems to be quite consistent with his conclusion. Wage inflation began to accelerate, only slightly and perhaps not permanently, when the actual unemployment rate fell below $5\frac{1}{2}$ percent and stayed there for a while.

This is about as good a case for accelerationism as one could make. In contrast with the European experience, it does not require any embarrassing shift in the natural rate to accommodate the hard facts. European economists, in attempting to save the natural-rate theory in the face of a long period of unusually high unemployment without any serious accompanying disinflation, often seem to be arguing

that the "natural" rate *must* have increased a lot precisely *because* wage inflation is not decelerating. That may be true, I suppose, but to argue that way empties the theory of all meaning. European experience can only be taken as evidence against the meaningfulness of a stable and well-defined natural rate. I will come back to that in a moment.

The question I want to raise now is whether the US evidence, as mobilized by Nichols, is actually very strong. What would an alternative theory of the labor market say about the acceleration of wage inflation? For instance, what would the general view I have been so temperately propagating have to say? Nothing very precise, of course: I have not proposed any very tight theory, only a class of theories. Presumably, however, one implication is that steady inflation could be associated with a range of unemployment rates, not with a unique unemployment rate. If the labor market can be in equilibrium anywhere in an interval of unemployment rates and with an interval of real wage rates, then more or less steady wage and price inflation ought not to disturb that state of affairs very much.

In order to heighten the contrast with the natural-rate doctrine, I have tried out on the US data the hypothesis that inflation accelerates whenever the unemployment rate goes below its average for the past 5 years and decelerates whenever the unemployment rate exceeds its average for the past 5 years. Another way to put this is to say that any unemployment rate can play the role of the natural

rate if only it has persisted long enough, say for 5 years.

Now clearly this is much too strong. I do not believe that 5 years of 2 percent unemployment in the United States would permit the accompanying rate of inflation to stabilize. I have to say that I do not know what would happen in that case, but I would certainly not be surprised if the result were runaway inflation. I want to make it plain that I am not trying to fine-tune a hypothesis to the data themselves. There is already too much of that going on. Instead I want to compare one sharp hypothesis (that the "natural" rate of unemployment is more or less constant) with another (that the "natural" rate of unemployment can be almost anything the labor market has grown accustomed to).

My procedure is simply to replicate Nichols's work using essentially the same data: wage acceleration and unemployment in the United States from the end of the Korean War to the present, omitting, as he did, only the two OPEC-inspired bursts of inflation in the 1970s. Then I ask: how well do the same data support the altogether different hypothesis that wage acceleration more or less vanishes whenever the unemployment rate is about where it has been for the past 5 years? The answer is: almost, but not quite, as well. The standard natural-rate hypothesis provides a slightly better statistical fit. Taken literally it confirms Nichols's estimate of the natural rate at just under $5\frac{1}{2}$ percent. But the "wandering-natural-rate" story trails only a little way

behind, and offers evidence that it is not missing anything systematic in the explanation of wage acceleration.

Perhaps I should include a bit of detail here. If I regress the acceleration of average hourly earnings on the unemployment rate and a linear trend, the trend is not quite statistically significant, and in any case small. With or without it I get Nichols's result that the natural rate of unemployment is just under $5\frac{1}{2}$ percent. The regression explains about 65 percent of the variance in wage acceleration. The same sort of regression, with the unemployment rate replaced by its deviation from a 5-year moving average, explains about 53 percent of the variance. The trend term is statistically significant this time, suggesting a decrease in wage acceleration. Without the trend the fit is slightly less close, but the constant term is very close to zero, as it ought to be. I will add one further detail. If I replace average hourly earnings by the more inclusive and theoretically more appropriate series for average hourly "compensation," the qualitative story is the same. But the fit of the regression is worse in both cases and the margin between them narrows a lot.

I want to underline the fact that I have fought off the temptation to improve the fit by doctoring here and there. Another time, with other data, that might be a worthwhile exercise. I have already mentioned that the wandering-natural-rate hypothesis has been used in a form far too uncompromising to be credible. I would be entitled to trim the hypothesis at very low and very high unemployment rates. To

take another example, I chose a 5-year average as an estimate of the wandering natural rate because I have five fingers on each hand, not as the result of a statistical search. Even the idea of a moving average is only the most primitive way to capture the spirit of the underlying theory. There must be better formulations. The 5-year moving average was intended to embody the idea that any reasonable unemployment rate, accompanied by a productivity-based real-wage trend, could become the norm; only a major departure from the norm would occasion a breakdown of the consensual behavior that maintains the norm. But the statistical use of a 5-year moving average asserts something stronger and less credible: that an unemployment rate fluctuating widely on both sides of x percent has the same norm-building properties as an unemployment rate confined within a narrow band around x percent. That does not sound right at all. There are straightforward ways to correct that distortion of the underlying thought. I have not pursued them now because my purpose is to cast doubt, not to solicit belief.

My tentative conclusion is this. The United States is perhaps the best case to be found among advanced industrial economies to support the idea of a single stable equilibrium unemployment rate (in the accelerationist sense). However, there turns out to be only weak support for this now standard view of the labor market as against the alternative view that labor-market behavior is largely norm guided. Even the simplest representation of the alternative view can give nearly as good an account of the US data.

There is adequate reason to believe that it could be improved by the sort of tuning that, for better or worse, is the daily routine of econometrics.

As I have indicated, Europe provides an altogether different picture. Attempts to salvage the idea of a well-defined equilibrium unemployment rate require the equilibrium rate itself to have undergone drastic change between the 1970s and the 1980s. To any reasonably skeptical person, it all smacks of the invocation of epicycles to salvage Ptolemaic astronomy, but apparently with rather less success.

I have not tried to apply any model of a norm-guided labor market to European data. One already knows from the gross facts that it would do better than a natural-rate theory that was not allowed to juggle the natural rate itself. No purpose would be served by fishing in those waters. I can cite two empirical studies, however, that were done without any particular theoretical alternative in mind.

One is by Robert J. Gordon of Northwestern University. His analytical framework is very different from mine in detail, and I shall not try here to reconcile them. But his conclusion is easy to state. He finds that the acceleration of wage inflation in Europe depends not on the state of the economy but on the *change* in the state of the economy. In other words, Gordon's conclusion is that wage inflation in the OECD accelerates when the economy is improving, not simply when it is good. Translated roughly into the terms I have been using, wage inflation accelerates when the unemployment rate is falling. It is almost as if the role of the "natural"

unemployment rate is played by last year's unemployment rate, or perhaps something just a little more complicated. There is no way of telling from Gordon's published results whether the moving-average model or something else suggested by norm-guided labor-market behavior would work well in Europe. It would certainly outperform the textbook story.

Finally I would like to mention a careful study by David Grubb of the London School of Economics and the OECD staff. Grubb's paper uses data for OECD countries through 1983, so some of the more embarrassing observations had not yet occurred when he did his work. His statistical calculations are within the natural-rate framework, rather like those of Nichols, but Grubb incorporates several additional explanatory variables to help account for wage acceleration in each of his countries. That makes detailed comparisons pointless. What is essential for me is that his equation for the United States does no better than the norm-guided moving-average model that I described earlier, maybe a little worse. Moreover Grubb's model fits other OECD countries no better, taking one with another, despite the additional variables. Indeed he is able to explain countries like France and Great Britain only by incorporating the hypothesis that the natural rate of unemployment is subject to an upward time trend.

I think it is a fair interim conclusion that the norm-guided approach to the labor market can do at least as well econometrically as the orthodox view in the European context, and almost as well in the

American context. If you will grant me any extra credit for conformity with common sense, then I think I am running just about even. That is all I hope for at this stage of the game.

Now I promised to say something about policies aimed at combating persistent unemployment. The beginning of good sense, however, is never to leap from broad theoretical constructions to concrete policy advice. What I can hope to do is something much more modest and (therefore?) maybe more interesting. If a model of the labor market were to be cobbled together out of the various elements I have been highlighting here, what would its general implications for policy be? What sorts of actions might it suggest that would tend to be buried on the more conventional view of labor-market equilibrium? Or is it all pretty much the same in practice?

The first thing to say is that there is good news and there is bad news. The good news is that the alternative model contains no implication that persistent high unemployment proclaims its own inevitability, barring major changes in institutions. In practice, that is what the accelerationist model says. On the alternative view, there is no general reason to presuppose that the current unemployment rate, even if it is an equilibrium unemployment rate, is the lowest achievable equilibrium unemployment rate. On the contrary, the odds are against that. Policy is entitled at least to experiment with the possibility of leading the economy and the labor market to an equilibrium with less unemployment.

The bad news is that it may be a costly experiment even if it succeeds in the end. For example, the simplistic model of a wandering equilibrium unemployment rate that I described a moment ago has the implication that moving from one unemployment rate to a lower one entails at least 5 years of accelerating inflation followed by steady inflation at the new higher rate. (There might be other ways of getting inflation down again, at least to where it was at the start, without another round of high unemployment. Then again there might not. To find out, one needs a model of the whole economy, not just the labor market.) It is easy to calculate numerically from such a model just what the cost would be. It turns out, in round numbers, that a reduction of one point in the US unemployment rate entails a permanent increase in the inflation rate of around a point or a point and a quarter. But I interject immediately that the simple statistical model is much too crude to support any such statement.

In the paper to which I have already referred, Gordon uses his own preferred model for OECD Europe to do a similar exercise. His result is qualitatively similar to the one I have just reported. The form of the calculation is different: he estimates that a permanent increase of $3\frac{1}{2}$ percentage points in the ratio of output to trend would lead after a decade to a permanent acceleration of inflation by 3 points a year. In neither case is the inflationary cost trivial. One's judgment about the wisdom of

moving in that direction depends on one's judgment about the value of an extra $3\frac{1}{2}$ percent of gross domestic product, or the value of the work performed by the marginal 1 percent of employed workers. Into that must be factored the chance that the policy would fail. The important thing is that the more institutional view of the labor market opens up possibilities that the standard view just suppresses.

There is a minor subtlety here. The preceding discussion sounds like a reversion to the old notion of a permanent trade-off between inflation and unemployment. But that is not the case at all. In the story I have just told, the permanent increase in inflation is the cost of getting from a high unemployment rate to a lower one, not the cost of being at a lower unemployment rate. Either unemployment rate is compatible with steady inflation at either rate; that is what the existence of a range of equilibria means. It is the transition that calls forth the permanent acceleration of inflation, at least in this admittedly over-simple model. Had history been different, no transition with its associated inflationary cost would have been needed. One lesson that emerges is the importance of not letting unemployment drift to the top of its equilibrium range in the first place. Once history matters, error is not costlessly reversible.

This distinction leads to an interesting point about policy options: it makes a new kind of case for incomes policies. The older case for an incomes policy foundered on the rock that a permanently effective incomes policy is hard to believe in, but a

permanently effective incomes policy is exactly what is needed given the older view of the Phillips curve. (If you believe in an effective natural rate of unemployment, incomes policy is a non-starter.) History offers us at best examples of incomes policies that work for a while and then crumble. When the goal is to reduce the unemployment rate from the top of an equilibrium range to the bottom, then a temporary incomes policy is exactly what the doctor ordered. If acceleration of inflation can be eliminated or reduced during the transition, then the situation at the end of the process should be just as viable as the situation at the beginning, as long as the unemployment rate stays in the equilibrium range.

Even temporarily effective incomes policies are hard to achieve in decentralized labor markets like our own. They might be easier in the large European economies, and they may be what the smaller north European economies actually have, in effect. This is hardly Utopia, but it may be a glimmering of hope.

In most of what I have just been saying it is implicit that the policy means in question are traditional expansionary fiscal and monetary policy. The question is merely how to estimate their consequences for wage (and price) inflation. A more exotic question is whether one might turn to rather different sorts of policy altogether to improve the performance of the labor market itself. Keep in mind that institutional reforms are not intended as a way of reducing currently high levels of unemployment, but rather as a way of shifting the

range of possible equilibrium unemployment rates downward.

Suppose, for example, that Lindbeck and Snower are right in emphasizing insider–outsider interactions in the maintenance of high equilibrium unemployment. Then a natural corrective would be to seek ways of amplifying the voice of outsiders in labor markets. There is a complication, however, the sort of complication that arises just because the labor market is a social institution and not a machine for matching supply and demand. It is one thing to strengthen the hand of outsiders relative to insiders and quite another to strengthen the hand of employers relative to insiders. Employment might rise in both cases, but the distributional implications could be different. (The political consequences are obviously different.) As a practical matter, reforms have a better chance of surviving if they do not, and do not seem to, take sides between employers and workers.

One easily acceptable initiative might be the establishment and formalization of apprenticeship programs. These are far more common in Europe than in the United States. (They are especially well developed in West Germany, and so obviously they do not by themselves guarantee the achievement of low unemployment rates.) The idea is both to provide a route to relevant skills besides on-the-job training, and to create some kind of formal association between incumbent workers and the external supply of labor. A more direct but also more complicated reform would be to provide for

the formal representation of outsiders in collective bargaining negotiations. It is not obvious how the relevant group of outsiders is to be defined, who should represent them, or how any such scheme could avoid being seen as a pure and simple increase in the bargaining power of employers. Perhaps a way can be found to induce or compel labor unions themselves to represent the unemployed part of the membership adequately, provided that membership is actually open. That is a good question to ask of specialists in industrial relations.

Efficiency–wage theory suggests a rather different class of labor-market reform. The commonest version of efficiency–wage theory claims that the average level of unemployment is as high as it is because the threat of discharge for cause has to be serious enough to elicit an efficient intensity of performance on the job. If the unemployment rate were any lower, jobs would be too easy to find, the threat of losing any given job would not occasion any great loss, and work effort would be less. Here too we have to pick our way carefully. If the ultimate source of unemployment is the difficulty of monitoring work effort directly, one can imagine all sorts of Big Brother schemes – one-way mirrors, paid snitches, pep pills – that might lower the equilibrium unemployment rate or rates. But that is a cure worse than the disease. The question is whether there are acceptable and equitable ways to achieve the desired goal.

Again two possible initiatives suggest themselves by way of example. Presumably the best possible

monitors of work effort are other workers in the same shop-floor group. If a major part of compensation for work were tied to group effort or group productivity, which must be easier to observe than individual effort and productivity, it would be in the interest of the group members to see that everyone contributed a fair share. The impulse to free-ride would certainly be latent, but the likelihood of getting away with it would be much less. There is some reason to believe – even apart from the effect that we are now discussing – that in American industry there is too little emphasis on teamwork and too much emphasis on individual performance for its own good, at all levels. If that is so, then there would be some additional benefit from incorporating an element of group compensation in pay schemes. There would also be some dangers, no doubt.

A second, rather obvious, idea is to look for ways to associate each worker's interest more directly with the success of the firm. Agreements tying wages to productivity are in use, here and elsewhere, but they have the limitation that the individual's productivity is not easily isolated and measured in the context of modern industry, including many service industries. Profit-sharing – or what is more broadly called gain-sharing – has some of the right properties. Once again there is an invitation to free-riding; but here too one could hope that the morale and discipline of the group would be enough to overcome the temptation. My colleague Martin Weitzman has urged on other grounds the advantages

of compensation schemes with a significant profit-sharing component. Maybe this is another route by which that device might help to lower the equilibrium unemployment rate.

The last suggestion I want to make is a sort of generalization of the others, and provides a summary note on which I can logically bring these lectures to an end. Earlier I proposed a way of resolving the puzzle of the supply side of the labor market, namely the rarity of active wage competition even under the stimulus of persistent unemployment. The proposal was that the social norm against "unfair" wage competition could emerge as reinforcement of a particular equilibrium choice of strategies for workers and firms. In that equilibrium, abstention from wage cutting is enforced by the latent threat of reversion to Hobbesian competition. The point I now want to make is that attempts to improve the working of the labor market by making it more nearly perfectly competitive may be misguided. They may be misguided in two ways: first because they might be resisted strongly and thus rendered impractical; and second because they may not be in the best interest of working people, who might be willing to pay a price to avoid having their livelihoods governed by atomistic competition.

This is a different way of stating the common-sense observation with which I began these lectures, that labor is not a commodity exactly like most others. It does not seem to me at all inconsistent or strange to suppose that a society might be happy to see fish or candy bars or computers traded in a

competitive market, but would rather not allocate and pay labor in quite the same way. It would then follow that the achievement of wage flexibility through unrestricted competition might not be the way to go. The question is whether we can tinker with labor-market institutions as I have suggested, or in other ways, so that they can provide the job security and wage continuity that people seem to want, without falling into gross inefficiency, and in particular into that grossest inefficiency – persistent unemployment.

Bibliographical Note

There is a vast literature on the determination of nominal wage rates. In volume and variety it rivals the literature on losing weight. As far as I know, the first suggestion that one could look directly at wage acceleration instead of the level or rate of change of the nominal wage came from Franco Modigliani and Lucas Papademos. See "Targets for Monetary Policy in the Coming Year," *Brookings Papers on Economic Activity*, volume 6, number 1 (1975), pages 141–66. The thought was recalled to me by the lucky accident that I was asked to be the discussant of a paper by Donald Nichols at the December 1987 convention of the American Economic Association. The paper, "The Decline of the Natural Rate of Unemployment," has not been published. I suppose it was felt to be *too* direct.

International comparisons, for all their problems, offer a way out of the mining of short one-country time series. An excellent example is "Topics in the OECD Phillips Curve," by David Grubb, *Economic Journal*, volume 96, number 1 (1986), pages 55–79. It takes wage acceleration as the independent variable, and adds a number of explanatory variables. There is ultimate value in this, although often the interpretation to be placed on the additional variables is open to dispute. I profited a lot, and even got some intellectual and moral support, from Robert J. Gordon's "Back to the Future: European Unemployment Today Viewed from America in 1939," *Brookings Papers on Economic Activity*, volume 19, number 1 (1988), pages 271–304. Gordon finds a rather distinct difference between contemporary United States and Europe.

A related but not identical view is to be found in the well-known paper by Olivier Blanchard and Lawrence Summers, "Hysteresis and the European Unemployment Problem," *NBER Macroeconomics Annual* (MIT Press, 1986), volume 1, pages 15–78.

After I had already delivered the lectures I received a working paper by Assar Lindbeck and Dennis Snower entitled "Macroeconomic Policy and Insider Power," Seminar Paper No. 429 of the Institute for International Economic Studies, University of Stockholm, January 1989. I was glad to find a substantial amount of overlap. I have also discovered a very useful paper by David Coe: "Hysteresis Effects in Aggregate Wage Equations," in *Unemployment, Hysteresis and the Natural Rate*

Hypothesis, edited by R. Cross (Blackwell, Oxford, 1988), pages 284–305. Coe tests the wandering natural rate against the conventional version for a number of countries. He estimates Phillips curves rather than the acceleration equations that I slightly prefer. His conclusions are very much like mine. The United States is among the less favorable candidates for the wandering-natural-rate hypothesis (although recent experience, not included, may tilt the results the other way). For several other countries, including Great Britain, the wandering rate may be slightly superior. For still others, there is little to choose. It is interesting how prior mindsets influence interpretations. I read Coe as saying: if the wandering natural rate is not clearly superior to the standard view, who needs it? My reaction is: if the conventional view is not clearly superior to alternatives, why is it uncritically taken for granted?

Appendix

A wage-acceleration equation can be derived in the following simple way. Let w_t be the logarithm of the nominal wage in year t, so that $w_t - w_{t-1} = z_t$ is the proportional rate of wage inflation. The simplest expectations-augmented Phillips curve would read

$$z_t = q - b\,(u_t - u^*) + p_t^e - p_{t-1}, \qquad (1)$$

where p_t^e is the logarithm of the expected price level for year t, conditional on all the information up to

and including year $t - 1$, so that $p_t^e - p_{t-1}$ is the expected rate of inflation. (The constant q is the relevant rate of productivity growth, defining a "neutral" rate of increase of the real wage.) Now suppose that (a) expectations simply extrapolate recent inflation, so that $p_t^e - p_{t-1} = p_{t-1} - p_{t-2}$, and (b) the price level is a constant mark-up on unit labor cost, so that $p_{t-1} - p_{t-2} = z_{t-1} - q$. Then (1) becomes

$$z_t - z_{t-1} = -b(u_t - u^*). \tag{2}$$

As promised, (2) is a straightforward acceleration equation: wage inflation accelerates whenever $u < u^*$ and decelerates whenever $u > u^*$. The only unemployment rate consistent with steady inflation is u^*, and it is compatible with inflation at any rate.

The admirable paper by Nichols referred to in the lecture estimates (2) using data on civilian unemployment and average hourly earnings adjusted for overtime and inter-industry shifts. The sample period is 1955–86, with the years 1974–5 and 1980–1 omitted as outliers under the influence of OPEC. I have replicated his calculation with results so close as to suggest that any difference may come from minor revisions of the data.

A representative regression is

$$z_t - z_{t-1} = 0.025 - 0.458u$$
$$(6.73) \quad (7.41)$$

$$(\bar{R}^2 = 0.65, \text{DW} = 2.1) \tag{3a}$$

(DW, Durbin–Watson) which implies that $u^* = 0.055$. When a linear time trend is added, it

is insignificant and the other coefficients are little changed:

$$z_t - z_{t-1} = 0.025 - 0.499u + 0.00011t$$
$$\phantom{z_t - z_{t-1} = } (6.82) \quad (6.36) \qquad (0.80)$$
$$(\bar{R}^2 = 0.67, \text{DW} = 2.2) \qquad \text{(3b)}$$

(The numbers in parentheses are t ratios.) When the more inclusive, and therefore presumably better, series for compensation of employees is used instead of average hourly earnings, the statistical quality deteriorates:

$$z_t - z_{t-1} = 0.029 - 0.512u$$
$$\phantom{z_t - z_{t-1} = } (4.06) \quad (4.24)$$
$$(\bar{R}^2 = 0.39, \text{DW} = 2.8) \qquad \text{(3c)}$$

$$z_t - z_{t-1} = 0.029 - 0.632u + 0.00033t$$
$$\phantom{z_t - z_{t-1} = } (4.08) \quad (4.13) \qquad (1.25)$$
$$(\bar{R}^2 = 0.40, \text{DW} = 2.85) \qquad \text{(3d)}$$

The implied u^* is now 0.057.

Of course u^* does not have to be a constant, and one talks easily about "changes in the natural rate of unemployment." But the story requires that u^* change seldom, or at least slowly and systematically. If it varies often and unpredictably, (2) has little explanatory value. Every year there must be some value of u^* that makes (2) true; but that is no help unless one knows in advance what the value is or what makes it what it is.

My game is to estimate equations corresponding to (3a)–(3d) with u^* replaced by $\bar{u}_t$ defined as $\frac{1}{5}(u_{t-1} + u_{t-2} + u_{t-3} + u_{t-4} + u_{t-5})$. This is an

extreme way of making u^* "unstructural," highly dependent on the path of the economy and on nothing else. I want to emphasize that $\bar{u}$ is a stalking-horse, not a literal hypothesis. I have deliberately not tuned it to the data. I did check to see that a 5-year moving average worked better than a 3-year moving average, but that is all. Obviously I could do "better" if I let the data choose a weighted moving average rather than an unweighted one, or if I let the data choose a nonlinear function of $u_t - \bar{u}_t$ rather than the simple difference. But that is a different game and one I do not like to play.

One finds

$$z_t - z_{t-1} = -0.00080 - 0.374\,(u_t - \bar{u}_t)$$
$$(0.340) \qquad (3.17)$$
$$(\bar{R}^2 = 0.38, \text{GLS}, \rho = 0.43) \qquad \text{(4a)}$$

$$z_t - z_{t-1} = -0.0091 - 0.401\,(u_t - \bar{u}_t) - 0.00045t$$
$$(2.48) \qquad (4.00) \qquad\qquad (2.92)$$
$$(\bar{R}^2 = 0.53, \text{GLS}, \rho = 0.21) \quad \text{(4b)}$$

$$z_t - z_{t-1} = 0.0011 - 0.585\,(u_t - \bar{u}_t)$$
$$(0.53) \qquad (3.58)$$
$$(\bar{R}^2 = 0.30, \text{DW} = 2.45) \qquad \text{(4c)}$$

$$z_t - z_{t-1} = 0.0093 - 0.597\,(u_t - \bar{u}_t) - 0.00038t$$
$$(1.87) \qquad (3.80) \qquad\qquad (1.80)$$
$$(\bar{R}^2 = 0.36, \text{DW} = 2.74) \qquad \text{(4d)}$$

(GLS, generalized least squares.)

Obviously, equations (4a)–(4d) do not provide as good a fit as the standard equations (3a)–(3d), nor would I expect them to. But it strikes me as sobering

that so drastic a deviation from the conventional view as this "wandering natural rate" requires so little sacrifice in the way of statistical success. Indeed in the case of (3d) and (4d), with the conceptually better measure of wage rates, there is actually little to choose. So powerful a statement about the economy as the existence of a single stable unemployment rate separating accelerating inflation from accelerating deflation ought to rest on more secure foundations.

If (2) is the correct model, the process of disinflation is easily described. Imagine the economy at $u = u^*$ but with an ongoing steady inflation. An increase in u by 0.01 for 1 year followed by a return to u^* will cause a permanent reduction in the rate of inflation by a fraction b of 1 percent per year (according to (3a), about 0.5 percent). Now suppose the correct model were

$$z_t - z_{t-1} = -a(u_t - \bar{u}_t). \tag{5}$$

Imagine the economy with a constant unemployment rate (so that $u_t = \bar{u}_t$) and, correspondingly, a constant rate of inflation. An increase in u by 0.01 maintained for 5 years will reduce inflation by the fraction a of 1 percent in the first year, because $u_t - \bar{u}_t = 0.01$. In the second year $\bar{u}_t$ will increase by 0.002 and wage inflation will decelerate by a fraction $0.8a$ of 1 percent. Third-year deceleration will be $0.6a$, followed by $0.4a$, $0.2a$, and then once again $u = \bar{u}$ and inflation stabilizes. But the economy is now stuck with the higher u. Thus the permanent increase

in u by 1 percent buys – after 5 years – a permanent reduction in inflation by $3a$ percent (according to (4a), a little over 1 percent). The difference between (5) and (2) is that (2) ties accelerating inflation to low unemployment, (5) to lower unemployment than lately. Probably life is more complicated than either.

This is not like natural-rate theory, but neither is it like the old Phillips curve trade-off. Path dependence, if you take it seriously, implies its own kind of world, but it is a world that has a logic of its own.

Works by
Robert M. Solow

1950

Review of *Economic Fluctuations in the U.S., 1921–1941*
by L. Klein, *Mechanical Engineering* (1950).
Review of *Labor Productivity Functions in Meat Packing*
by W. H. Nicholls, *Review of Economics and Statistics*
(August 1950).

1951

"A Note on Dynamic Multipliers." *Econometrica* 19,
no. 3 (July 1951): 306–16.
"Some Long-Run Aspects of the Distribution of Wage
Incomes." *Econometrica* 19, no. 3 (July 1951): 333–4.
Review of *Statistical Inference in Dynamic Economic
Models* edited by Tjalling C. Koopmans, *Review of
Economics and Statistics* 33, no. 4 (November 1951):
358–60.

1952

With Kenneth J. Arrow and Ronald W. Shephard,
abstract. "An Econometric Model of Interindustry
Material Flows." *Econometrica* 20, no. 3 (July 1952):
488–9.

"On the Structure of Linear Models." *Econometrica* 20, no. 1 (January 1952): 29–46.

Review of *Some Theory of Sampling* by William E. Deming, *Review of Economics and Statistics* 34, no. 2 (May 1952): 193–4.

Review of *Application of Linear Programming to the Theory of the Firm* by R. Dorfman, *Journal of American Statistical Association* (June 1952).

Review of *Activity Analysis of Production and Allocation* edited by Tjalling C. Koopmans, *American Economic Review* 42, no. 3 (June 1952): 424–9.

Review of *Cahiers du Séminaire d'Econométrie, No. 1* edited by R. Roy, *Journal of American Statistical Association* (December 1952).

1953

"A Note on the Price Level and Interest Rate in a Growth Model." *Review of Economic Studies* 21, no. 1 (1953): 74–9.

With Paul A. Samuelson. "Balanced Growth under Constant Returns to Scale." *Econometrica* 21, no. 3 (April 1953): 412–24.

Review of *A Textbook of Econometrics* by Lawrence R. Klein, *American Economic Review* 43, no. 5 (December 1953): 947–50.

1954

"A New Survey of Demand Analysis." *Review of Economics and Statistics* 36 (February 1954): 104–7.

"The Survival of Mathematical Economics." *Review of Economics and Statistics* 36 (November 1954): 372–4.

1955

Review of *A Study in the Theory of Economic Evolution* by Trygve Haavelmo, *American Economic Review* 45, no. 1 (March 1955): 155–6.

Review of *An Essay on the Economic Theory of Rank* by R. H. Tuck, *Journal of American Statistical Association* (September 1955).

Review of *Elements of Pure Economics* (English translation) by L. Walras, *Econometrica* (October 1955).

"The Production Function and the Theory of Capital." *Review of Economic Studies* 23, no. 2 (1955–6): 101–8.

1956

"A Contribution to the Theory of Economic Growth." *Quarterly Journal of Economics* 70, no. 1 (February 1956): 65–94.

Review of *The Analysis of Family Budgets* by S. Prais and H. S. Houthakker, *Journal of American Statistical Association* (June 1956): 398–400.

Review of *International Economic Papers No. 5* edited by Alan T. Peacock et al., *American Economic Review* 46, no. 5 (December 1956): 981–3.

With Paul A. Samuelson. "A Complete Capital Model Involving Heterogeneous Capital Goods." *Quarterly Journal of Economics* 70 (November 1956): 537–62.

1957

Review of *The Failure of Economics: A Diagnostic Study* by Sidney Schoeffler, *Review of Economics and Statistics* 39, no. 1 (February 1957): 96–8.

"Technical Change and the Aggregate Production Function." *Review of Economics and Statistics* 39, no. 3 (August 1957): 312–20.

Review of *Economic Growth and Instability* by D. Hamberg, *Econometrica* 25, no. 4 (October 1957): 612–13.

1958

With Kenneth J. Arrow. "Gradient Methods for Constrained Maxima with Weakened Assumptions." Chapter in *Studies in Linear and Nonlinear Programming*, Stanford, CA: Stanford University Press, 1958.

With Robert Dorfman and Paul A. Samuelson. *Linear Programming and Economic Analysis*, New York: McGraw-Hill,1958.

Review of *Models of Man – Social and Rational* by Herbert A. Simon, *Review of Economics and Statistics* 40, no. 1 (February 1958): 81–4.

"A Skeptical Note on the Constancy of Relative Shares." *American Economic Review* 48, no. 4 (September 1958): 618–31.

Review of *The Structural Interdependence of the Economy: Proceedings of an International Conference on Input–Output Analysis* edited by Tibor Barna, *Econometrica* 26, no. 1 (January 1958): 173–4.

Review of *Three Essays on the State of Economic Science* by Tjalling C. Koopmans, *Journal of Political Economy* 66 (April 1958): 178–9.

Review of *Lohnhöhe und Beschäftigung* by W. Krelle and H. Haller, *Econometrica* 26, no. 3 (July 1958): 475–6.

"Technical Progress and the Production Function: A Reply." *Review of Economics and Statistics* 40, no. 4 (November 1958): 411–13.

1959

"Competitive Valuation in a Dynamic Input–Output System." *Econometrica* 27, no. 1 (January 1959): 30–53.

"On Concepts and Measures of Changes in Productivity: Comment." *Review of Economics and Statistics* 41, no. 3 (August 1959): 282–5.

Review of *An Approach to the Theory of Income Distribution* by S. Weintraub, *Journal of Political Economy* 67, no. 4 (August 1959): 420–1.

"Is Factor Substitution a Crime and If So, How Bad? Reply to Professor Eisner." *Economic Journal* 69 (September 1959): 597–9.

"Investment and Economic Growth: Some Comments." *Productivity Measurement Review* (November 1959).

1960

"Income Inequality Since the War." Chapter in *Postwar Economic Trends in the United States*, New York: Harper and Brothers, 1960.

"On a Family of Lag Distributions." *Econometrica* 28, no. 2 (April 1960): 393–406.

With P. A. Samuelson. "Analytic Aspects of Anti-Inflation Policy." *American Economic Review (Papers and Proceedings)* 50, no. 2 (May 1960): 177–94.

"Investment and Technical Progress." Chapter in *Mathematical Methods in the Social Sciences, 1959*, Stanford, CA: Stanford University Press, 1960.

1961

"A Wicksellian Model of Distributive Shares." Chapter in *The Theory of Capital: Proceedings of a Conference held at the International Economic Association*, New York: Macmillan, 1961.

"Note on Uzawa's Two-Sector Model of Economic Growth." *Review of Economic Studies* 29 (October 1961): 48–50.

"Education, Technology, and the GNP." *Technology Review* 63 (April 1961): 17–19, 34, 36.

With Kenneth J. Arrow, Hollis B. Chenery, and Bagicha S. Minhas. "Capital–Labor Substitution and Economic Efficiency." *Review of Economics and Statistics* 43, no. 3 (August 1961): 225–50.

1962

"Economic Growth and Housing." Chapter in *1962 Proceedings: Conference on Savings and Residential Financing*, New York: US Savings and Loan League, 1962, pp. 118–47.

"Some Problems of the Theory and Practice of Economic Planning." *Economic Development and Cultural Change* 10, no. 2, pt 1 (January 1962): 216–22.

"Technical Progress, Capital Formation, and Economic Growth." *American Economic Review (Papers and Proceedings)* 52, no. 2 (May 1962): 76–86.

"Substitution and Fixed Proportions in the Theory of Capital." *Review of Economic Studies* 29 (June 1962): 207–18.

"Problems that Don't Worry Me." *Technology Review* (July 1962): 43–4, 64.

"Investment for Growth." *New Republic* (20 October 1962): 14–15.

"A Policy for Full Employment." *Industrial Relations* 2, no. 1 (October 1962): 1–14.

Review of *Productivity and Technical Change* by W. E. G. Salter, *Review of Economics and Statistics* 44, no. 4 (November 1962): 501–2.

1963

Capital Theory and the Rate of Return (F. DeVries Lectures), Amsterdam: North-Holland, 1963.

With Albert Ando, E. Cary Brown, and John Kareken. "Lags in Fiscal and Monetary Policy." Chapter in *Stabilization Policies*, Englewood Cliffs, NJ: Prentice-Hall, 1963.

"Heterogeneous Capital and Smooth Production Functions: An Experimental Study." *Econometrica* 31, no. 4 (October 1963): 623–45.

1964

The Nature and Sources of Unemployment in the United States (Wicksell Lectures 1964), Stockholm: Almqvist and Wicksell, 1964.

"Capital, Labor and Income in Manufacturing." Chapter in *The Behavior of Income Shares: Selected Theoretical and Empirical Issues*, Princeton, NJ: Princeton University Press, 1964.

"Friedman on America's Money." *Banker* 114 (November 1964): 710–17.

1965

"Economic Behaviour Under Uncertainty" (Royal Society Nuffield Lecture). Chapter in *Proceedings of the Royal Society, Series B*, 162 (1965): 444–57.

1966

"The Case Against the Case Against the Guideposts." Chapter in *Guidelines, Informal Controls and the Market Place*, Chicago, IL: Chicago University Press, 1966.

"The Wage–Price Issue and the Guideposts." Chapter in *Critical Issues in Employment Policy*, Princeton, NJ: Princeton University Press, 1966.

With J. Tobin, C. C. von Weizsäcker, and M. Yaari. "Neoclassical Growth with Fixed Factor Proportions." *Review of Economic Studies* 33, no. 2 (April 1966): 79–115.

1967

With Malcolm S. Cohen. "The Behavior of Help-Wanted Advertising." *Review of Economics and Statistics* 49, no. 1 (February 1967): 108–10.

"The New Industrial State or Son of Affluence: Discussion and Rejoinder." *The Public Interest* no. 9 (Fall 1967): 100–8, 118–19.

"The Interest Rate and Transition Between Techniques." Chapter in *Socialism, Capitalism and Economic Growth*, Cambridge: Cambridge University Press, 1967.

"Some Recent Developments in the Theory of Production." Chapter in *The Theory and Empirical Analysis of Production*, New York: National Bureau of Economic Research, 1967.

1968

"Short-Run Adjustment of Employment to Output." Chapter in *Value, Capital and Growth: Papers in Honour of Sir John Hicks*, Edinburgh: Edinburgh University Press, 1968.

"Distribution in the Long and Short Run." Chapter in *The Distribution of National Income*, London: Macmillan, 1968.

"Recent Controversy on the Theory of Inflation: An Eclectic View." Chapter in *Inflation: Causes, Consequences and Control*, Wilton, CT: Kazanjian Economics Foundation, 1968.

"The Truth Further Refined: A Comment on Marris." *The Public Interest* no. 11 (Spring 1968): 47–52.

With Joseph E. Stiglitz. "Output, Employment and Wages in the Short Run." *Quarterly Journal of Economics* 82, no. 4 (November 1968): 537–60.

1969

Price Expectations and the Behavior of the Price Level (University of Manchester Lectures), Manchester: Manchester University Press, 1969.

1970

Growth Theory: An Exposition (The Radcliffe Lectures 1969), New York: Oxford University Press, 1970.

"On the Rate of Return: Reply to Pasinetti." *Economic Journal* 80 (June 1970): 423–8.

"Science and Ideology in Economics." *The Public Interest* no. 21 (Fall 1970): 94–107.

With Malcolm S. Cohen. "The Behavior of Help-Wanted Advertising: A Reply." *Review of Economics and Statistics* 52, no. 4 (November 1970): 442–3.

With Joseph E. Stiglitz. "Solow and Stiglitz on Employment and Distribution: A New Romance with an Old Model?: Reply." *Quarterly Journal of Economics* 84, no. 1 (February 1970): 153.

1971

Review of *The Gift Relationship: From Human Blood to Social Policy* by Richard M. Titmuss, *Yale Law Journal* 80, no. 8 (July 1971): 1696–1711.

"The Economist's Approach to Pollution and Its Control." *Science* (6 August 1971): 498–503. Reprinted in *Social Science* 47, no. 1 (Winter 1972): 15–25.

"Kuznets is Termed the Father of the G.N.P." *New York Times* (16 October 1971): 2.

With William S. Vickrey. "Land Use in a Long Narrow City." *Journal of Economic Theory* 3, no. 4 (December 1971): 430–47.

"Some Implications of Alternative Criteria for the Firm." Chapter in *The Corporate Economy: Growth, Competition and Innovative Potential*, Cambridge, MA: Harvard University Press, 1971.

"The State of Economics: The Behavioral and Social Sciences Survey: Discussion." *American Economic Review (Papers and Proceedings)* 61, no. 2 (May 1971): 63–5.

"Solow Prices and the Dual Stability Paradox in the Leontief Dynamic System: Comment." *Econometrica* 39, no. 3 (May 1971): 633–4.

1972

"Congestion, Density and the Use of Land in Transportation." *Swedish Journal of Economics* 74, no. 1 (March 1972): 161–73.

"The Economics of Pollution." Speech given at San Francisco Conference on *Jobs and the Environment* (28 November 1972).

"Notes on 'Doomsday Models'." *Proceedings of the National Academy of Sciences* 69, no. 12 (December 1972): 3832–3.

1973

"On Equilibrium Models of Urban Location." Chapter in *Essays in Modern Economics*, London: Longman, 1973.

Review of *Affluence and its Enemies* by Peter Passell and Leonard Ross, *New York Times Book Review* (25 February 1973): 4.

"Is the End of the World at Hand?" *Challenge* 16, no. 1 (March–April 1973): 39–50.

"What Happened to Full Employment?" *The Quarterly Review of Economics and Business* 13, no. 2 (Summer 1973): 7–20.

"Congestion Cost and the Use of Land for Streets." *Bell Journal of Economics and Management Science* 4, no. 2 (Autumn 1973): 602–18.

With Alan S. Blinder. "Does Fiscal Policy Matter?" *Journal of Public Economics* 2, no. 4 (November 1973): 319–37.

"Resource Scarcity and Economic Growth." *Hearings of Subcommittee on Priorities and Economy in Government of Joint Economic Committee* (20 December 1973).

"A Comment on Some Uses of Mathematical Models in Urban Economics: Rejoinder – I." *Urban Studies* 10, no. 2 (June 1973): 267.

"Some Evidence on the Short-Run Productivity Puzzle." Chapter in *Development and Planning: Essays in Honour of Paul Rosenstein Rodan*. Cambridge, MA: MIT Press, 1973.

1974

With Eli Ginzberg. "An Introduction to this Special Issue." *The Public Interest* no. 34 (Winter 1974): 4–13.

With Eli Ginzberg. "Some Lessons of the 1960s." *The Public Interest* no. 34 (Winter 1974): 211–20.

"What Do We Owe to the Future?" *Nebraska Journal of Economics and Business* 13, no. 1 (Winter 1974): 3–16.

"The Economics of Resources or the Resources of Economics." *American Economic Review (Papers and Proceedings)* 64, no. 2 (May 1974): 1–14.

"Intergenerational Equity and Exhaustible Resources." *Review of Economic Studies* 41 (Symposium) (1974): 29–45.

Review of *Capital and Time. A Neo-Austrian Theory* by John Hicks, *The Economic Journal* 84 (March 1974): 189–92.

"Law of Production and Laws of Algebra: The Humbug Production Function: A Comment." *The Review of Economics and Statistics* 56, no. 1 (February 1974): 121.

"Energy Crisis and the Environment." *The Catalyst* (12 April 1974): 5.

With Alan S. Blinder. "Analytical Foundations of Fiscal Policy." Chapter in *The Economics of Public Finance*, Washington, DC: Brookings Institution, 1974.

"The Management of Exhaustible Resources." Chapter in *Towards a Plan of Actions for Mankind*, Amsterdam: North-Holland, 1974.

Edited with Eli Ginzberg. *The Great Society: Lessons for the Future*, New York: Basic Books, 1974.

1975

"Reswitching: Brief Comments." *Quarterly Journal of Economics* 89, no. 1 (February 1975): 48–52.

"The Intelligent Citizen's Guide to Inflation." *The Public Interest* no. 38 (Winter 1975): 30–66.

1976

"Down the Phillips Curve with Gun and Camera." Chapter in *Inflation, Trade and Taxes: Essays in*

Honor of Alice Bourneuf, Columbus, OH: Ohio State University Press, 1976.

With Frederic Y. Wan. "Extraction Costs in the Theory of Exhaustible Resources." *Bell Journal of Economics* 7, no. 2 (Autumn 1976): 359–70.

"Macro-policy and Full Employment." Chapter in *Jobs for Americans*, Englewood Cliffs, NJ: Prentice-Hall, 1976.

With Alan S. Blinder. "Does Fiscal Policy Still Matter?" *Journal of Monetary Economics* 2, no. 4 (November 1976): 506–10.

"Optimal Fishing with a Natural Predator." Chapter in *Public and Urban Economics: Essays in Honor of William S. Vickrey*, Lexington, MA: Lexington Books, 1976.

With Alan S. Blinder. "Does Fiscal Policy Matter? A Correction." *Journal of Public Economics* 5, nos 1–2 (January–February 1976): 183–4.

1977

"The Economics of Pollution Control." *ILO Report* 19, no. 2 (Spring 1977): 14–17.

"Requiem for a Rebate." *The New Republic* (7 May 1977): 11–13.

"Monopoly, Uncertainty, and Exploration." Chapter in *Natural Resources, Uncertainty and General Equilibrium Systems: Essays in Memory of Rafael Lusky*, New York: Academic Press, 1977.

Review of *Swindling and Selling: The Spanish Prisoner and Other Bargains* by Arthur A. Leff, *Bell Journal of Economics* 8, no. 2 (1977): 627–9.

With Alan S. Blinder. "Does Fiscal Policy Matter? The View from the Government Budget Restraint: A Reply." *Public Finance* 32, no. 3 (1977): 390–2.

With Franklin M. Fisher and James M. Kearl. "Aggregate Production Functions: Some CES Experiments." *Review of Economic Studies* 44, no. 2 (June 1977): 305–20.

1978

"What We Know and Don't Know About Inflation" (adaptation of the Killian Lectures given at Massachusetts Institute of Technology in 1977–8). *Technology Review* 81, no. 3 (December 1978/January 1979): 30–44.

With Martin N. Baily. "Public Service Employment as Macroeconomic Policy." Chapter in *Job Creation Through Public Service Employment*, Washington, DC: National Commission for Manpower Policy, 1978.

"Resources and Economic Growth." *American Economist* 22, no. 2 (Fall 1978): 5–11.

1979

"Alternative Approaches to Macroeconomic Theory: A Partial View" (text of the W. A. Mackintosh Lecture given at Queen's University, Kingston, Ontario, in March 1979). *Canadian Journal of Economics* 12, no. 3 (August 1979): 339–54.

"Another Possible Source of Wage Stickiness." *Journal of Macroeconomics* 1, no. 1 (Winter 1979): 79–82.

Review of *Stability and Inflation* edited by A. R. Bergstrom, A. J. L. Catt, M. H. Peston, and B. D. J. Silverstone, *Economics* 46 (August 1979): 310–11.

Review of *The Political Economy of Inflation* edited by F. Hirsch and J. Goldthorpe, *Journal of Interdisciplinary History* (1979): 547–9.

1980

"Employment Policy in Inflationary Times." Chapter in *Employing the Unemployed*, New York: Basic Books, 1980.

"What to Do (Macroeconomically) when OPEC Comes." Chapter in *Rational Expectations and Economic Policy*, Chicago: IL: University of Chicago Press, 1980.

"On Theories of Unemployment." *American Economic Review* 70, no. 1 (March 1980): 1–11.

The Story of a Social Experiment and Some Reflections (1980 Geary Lecture), Dublin: Economic and Social Research Institute, 1980.

"Inflated Tales." *Executive* (Cornell University, Graduate School of Business and Public Administration) 6, no. 3 (Summer 1980): 2–3, 50–4.

"Why Do We Feel So Bad?" Chapter in *The Economy: Three Views*, Memphis, TN: Southwestern University, 1980.

"Toward Realism about Inflation." Chapter in *Introductory Macroeconomics, 1980–81: Readings on Contemporary Issues*, Ithaca, NY, and London: Cornell University Press, 1980.

"Policy Responses to the Productivity Slowdown: Discussion." *The Decline in Productivity Growth: Proceedings of a Conference held at Edgartown, Massachusetts, June 1980*, Federal Reserve Bank of Boston, Conference Series, no. 22 (1980): 173–7.

1981

With Ian M. McDonald. "Wage Bargaining and Employment." *American Economic Review* 71, no. 5 (December 1981): 896–908.

Review of *Profitability and Employment* by Edmond Malinvaud, *Journal of Economic Literature* 19 (June 1981): 572–3.

Review of *Prices and Quantities: A Macroeconomic Analysis* by Arthur M. Okun, *The Public Interest* no. 65 (Fall 1981): 91–102.

1982

"Some Lessons from Growth Theory." Chapter in *Financial Economics: Essays in Honor of Paul Cootner*, Englewood Cliffs, NJ: Prentice-Hall, 1982.

"On the Lender of Last Resort." Chapter in *Financial Crises: Theory, History and Policy*, Cambridge: Cambridge University Press, 1982.

"Where Have All the Flowers Gone? Economic Growth in the 1960s." Chapter in *Economics in the Public Service: Papers in Honor of Walter W. Heller*, New York: W. W. Norton, 1982.

"Reflections on Saving Behavior." Chapter in *Saving and Government Policy*, Boston, MA: Federal Reserve Bank of Boston, 1982.

"Does Economics Make Progress?" *Bulletin of American Academy of Arts and Sciences* 36, no. 3 (December 1982): 11–31.

"The Economics Major: What It Is and What It Should Be: Panel Discussion." *American Economic Review* 72, no. 2 (May 1982): 139.

1983

"Keynes and the Management of Real National Income and Expenditure: Comment." Chapter in *Keynes and the Modern World: Proceedings of the Keynes Centenary Conference, King's College, Cambridge*, Cambridge: Cambridge University Press, 1983.

"Macroconfusion: The Dilemmas of Economic Policy: Comment." Chapter in *Macroeconomics, Prices and Quantities: Essays in Memory of Arthur M. Okun*, Washington, DC: Brookings Institution, 1983.

"Conversations with Neo-Keynesian Economists: The 'Older Generation'." Interview by Arjo Klamer. *Conversations with Economists: New Classical Economists and Opponents Speak Out on the Current Controversy in Macroeconomics*, Totowa, NJ: Rowan & Allanheld, 1983.

"Implications of the Government Deficit for U.S. Capital Formation: Discussion." Chapter in *The Economics of Large Government Deficits: Proceedings of a Conference Held at Melvin Village, New Hampshire, October 1983*, Boston, MA: Federal Reserve Bank of Boston, 1983.

Edited with E. Cary Brown. *Paul Samuelson and Modern Economic Theory*, New York: McGraw-Hill, 1983.

"Leif Johansen (1930–1982): A Memorial." *Scandinavian Journal of Economics* 85, no. 4 (1983): 445–59.

"Economic Development and the Development of Economics: Discussion." *World Development* 11, no. 10 (October 1983): 891–3.

"U.S. Labor Markets: Imbalance, Wage Growth, and Productivity in the 1970s: Comments and Discussion." *Brookings Papers on Economic Activity* 1 (1983): 123–8.

"Teaching Economics in the 1980s." *Journal of Economic Education* 14, no. 2 (Spring 1983): 65–8.

1984

"Mr. Hicks and the Classics." *Oxford Economic Papers, New Series* 36, supplement (November 1984): 13–25.

With Ian M. McDonald. "Union Wage Policies: Reply."
American Economic Review 74, no. 4 (September
1984): 759–61.

1985

With Ian M. McDonald. "Wages and Employment in
a Segmented Labor Market." *Quarterly Journal of
Economics* 100, no. 4 (November 1985): 1115–41.

"Reflections on Macroeconomic Modelling: Confessions
of a DRI Addict." *Eastern Economic Journal* 11, no. 1
(January–March 1985): 79–83.

"Insiders and Outsiders in Wage Determination." *Scandinavian Journal of Economics* 87, no. 2 (1985): 411–28.

"Manufacturing Wage Dispersion: An End Game
Interpretation: Comment." *Brookings Papers on Economic Activity* (1985): 107–10.

"Economic History and Economics." *American Economic
Review (Papers and Proceedings)* 75, no. 2 (May 1985):
328–31.

1986

"What Is a Nice Girl Like You Doing in a Place Like
This? Macroeconomics after Fifty Years." *Eastern
Economic Journal* 12, no. 3 (July–September 1986):
191–8.

"Unemployment: Getting the Questions Right." *Economica* 53, supplement (1986): S23–34.

"On the Intergenerational Allocation of Natural
Resources." *Scandinavian Journal of Economics* 88,
no. 1 (November 1986): 141–9.

"The Unemployment of Nations." *Business Economics*
21, no. 1 (January 1986): 5–12.

"Monopolistic Competition and the Multiplier." Chapter
in *Equilibrium Analysis: Essays in Honor of Kenneth*

J. Arrow, volume II, Cambridge: Cambridge University Press, 1986.

1987

"What Do We Know that Francis Amasa Walker Didn't?" *History of Political Economy*, 19, no. 2 (Summer 1987): 183–9.

"James Meade at Eighty." *Economic Journal* 97 (December 1987): 986–8.

"The Conservative Revolution: a Roundtable Discussion." *Economic Policy* (October 1987): 181–5.

1988

"The Wide Wide World of Wealth." Review of *The New Palgrave Dictionary of Economics*, edited by J. Eatwell, M. Milgate and P. Newman, *New York Times Book Review* (20 March 1988): 3, 25.

"Comments from Inside Economics." Chapter in *The Consequences of Economic Rhetoric*. Cambridge: Cambridge University Press, 1988.

"Growth Theory and After" (Nobel Lecture). *American Economic Review* 78, no. 3 (June 1988): 307–17.

1989

"Faith, Hope and Clarity." Chapter 4 in *The Spread of Economic Ideas*, Cambridge: Cambridge University Press, 1989.

"How Economic Ideas Turn to Mush." Chapter 7 in *The Spread of Economic Ideas*, Cambridge: Cambridge University Press, 1989.

Name Index

Subject Index

D1594289